THE ELEMENTS OF
LEGAL WRITING

THE ELEMENTS OF LEGAL WRITING

Martha Faulk and Irving M. Mehler

Macmillan • USA

MACMILLAN
A Simon & Schuster Macmillan Company
1633 Broadway
New York, NY 10019

A catalog record is available from the Library of Congress

ISBN 0-02-860839-9

Designed by Nancy Sugihara
10 9 8 7 6 5 4 3 2 1
Printed in the United States of America

To my parents, Madge and Jim
M.F.

To my wife, my children, and my grandchildren
I.M.M.

Contents

7 Principles of Capitalization 83

Acknowledgments

During the years that we have been in the legal profession, we have been helped and inspired by many people. We gratefully acknowledge all the law students, law professors, lawyers, judges, clerks, legal secretaries, and paralegals who have asked the questions and argued the points that inspired us to write this book. We appreciate the willingness of our friends and colleagues to provide many of the examples of legal writing that we've used to illustrate our rules.

We are especially grateful to Jan Morgan for her tireless and efficient preparation of the manuscript. We are also indebted to Raymond Hogler and Gordon Mehler for their perceptive editorial comments. Our special thanks go to our agent, Alison Brown Cerier, for representing us, and to our editor, Natalie P. Chapman, for bringing the project to its completion.

THE ELEMENTS OF
LEGAL WRITING

Introduction

In his famous novel *Bleak House,* Charles Dickens criticizes the complexity and obscurity of the British legal system. Dickens's brilliant opening scene describes the murky fog enveloping the City of London. He then compares the natural fog to the "fog" of the Chancery Court:

> Never can there come fog too thick, never can there come mud and mire too deep, to assort with the groping and floundering condition which this High Court of Chancery, most pestilent of hoary sinners, holds, this day, in the sight of heaven and earth.

Dickens's image of legal mystification unfortunately persists today. But for many reasons, important changes in legal writing are taking place.

Pressure to Reform

Legal language is undergoing a subtle but progressive reformation in law offices, courts, legislative committees, and corporate headquarters all across the country. Lawyers, paralegals, and legal secretaries are rethinking the way they draft contracts, construct pleadings and motions, and write to clients. This reform—like all change—is painful and often difficult for those involved, but it's an essential response to today's evolving legal profession.

Plain English Statutes

In the 1980s, many states reacted to public pressure to demystify the legal language used in consumer contracts and passed "plain English" statutes. In states such as Maine, Connecticut, New York, and Minnesota, lawyers dealing with consumer contracts and loans must write these documents in plain English, and other states require plain English in insurance policies.

When dealing with such varied subjects as building codes, tax instructions, legislative summaries, and ballot issues, lawyers employed by state governments are required to write documents in plain English. And lawyers working with federal legislation, the Uniform Commercial Code, or the Truth in Lending Act, for example, must also be aware of plain English issues.

"A Short and Plain Statement"

The judiciary has long been aware of the verbosity that besieges it. Commentators on the state of legal language relate the story of the seventeenth-century judge so outraged by the length of a brief that he cut a hole in the middle and hung it around the neck of the lawyer who wrote it.

A more modern example of a judicial penalty occurred in a Florida case. Lawyers who litigate in federal courts are aware of the requirement of "a short and plain statement of the claim" set forth in Rule 8 of the Federal Rules of Civil Procedure.

Dismissing a complaint full of "chaotic legal jargon," the federal appeals court cited the appellants' failure to comply with the requirement:

> The various complaints, amendments, amended amendments, amendments to amended amendments, and other related papers are anything but short, totaling over 4,000 pages, occupying 18 volumes, and requiring a hand truck or cart to move. They are not plain, either. (Gordon v. Green, 602 F.2d 743, 744-745 [5th Cir. 1979])

Perhaps the court's order requiring the four thousand pages to be worn around counsel's neck would also have been effective.

The Conservative Tradition

The language of the law has always had great power over the lives of ordinary citizens. With little understanding of how legal language has evolved over time, lawyers are often reluctant to change the way they write and think about the law, perhaps because they're reluctant to tamper with the source of power. Consequently, an understanding of how legal language has developed is the essential starting place for improvement.

Irving Younger, in his "Persuasive Writing" column for the *ABA Journal* (July 1986), blames much of the wordiness of legal writing upon a "military accident." That accident was the death of Harold Godwineson, a Saxon king killed by an arrow through his eye. Harold's defeat at Hastings in 1066 insured the Norman conquest of England, and thus our already voluble ancestors at the bar took up the French language of the Norman conquerors and added it to the rich Anglo-Saxon vocabulary. This amalgamation of Anglo-Saxon and French with Latin produced many words for virtually the same thing. These synonyms, sometimes called "doublings" and "triplings," remain with us today. Although they masquerade as separate, distinctive concepts, too often they are merely redundant.

History has given us other linguistic handicaps for clarity and precision. We've inherited many archaic words and phrases that clutter up the pages of contracts, briefs, pleadings, motions, and statutes. This legalese may appear to have legal significance but is usually too imprecise to be helpful to the reader. And to add to the legal babble, there are hundreds of archaic words and phrases that have little relevance to the modern world. Latin, for example, is rarely studied today, and many traditional Latin phrases have perfectly good English equivalents.

Economic Self-Interest

Despite one Harvard Law School professor's assertion that "lawyers write badly because doing so promotes their economic interests," we believe the opposite to be true. We've seen a growing interest in legal writing seminars for practicing attorneys and judges. Law schools, too, are revamping their legal writing programs to include professional instruction.

A glance through periodicals written for the legal profession reveals many "how to" articles on improving writing skills. The journal *Clarity*, devoted entirely to helping lawyers in Great Britain write understandable English, was developed in 1982 in response to a surveyor's plea to solicitors for comprehensible leases. In addition, many legal writing manuals have been published in recent years.

The most compelling argument for good writing is simply the legal process itself. Because the practice of law is inherently adversarial, lawyers care very much about winning. Certainly every lawyer knows that the ability to persuade on paper is an essential asset. But lawyers also know there are many impediments, peculiar to the legal profession, that cause much stumbling and rambling along the path to good writing. We've designed this book with these impediments in mind. Our comprehensive table of contents gives you a detailed overview of the various subjects covered. Our rules reflect modern English usage. And our examples are drawn from actual legal writing wherever possible. A glossary of grammatical terms is also provided to help you with unfamiliar words.

Since the large-scale organization of legal documents is beyond the scope of this book, we've included many excellent sources for discussion of the relationship between legal analysis and legal writing. The list of "Recommended Sources" provides a variety of books and articles containing explanations and examples of good legal memoranda, appellate briefs, advisory letters, and contracts.

1

Principles of Clear Writing

The ten rules set forth in this chapter provide a capsule review of how to write readable and persuasive legal language.

You're probably conversant with these precepts for good writing, but perhaps you've drifted away from them after reading and hearing too much convoluted legal prose.

⚔ Rule 1. Use short sentences for complicated thoughts.

Too often, legal writers include several important ideas in one long, complex sentence. The result is confusion and misunderstanding on the part of the reader. At the very least, the reader may be forced to reread the sentence.

Consider this example from an appellate brief, in which the writer is attempting to persuade the court that the district court made a mistake of interpretation.

> The district court, on the other hand, erroneously addressed but one word of the Bankers Blanket Bond—the term "realized"—and then the district court misapplied it by erroneously considering whether [the appellee] "realized" a benefit and the Bank suffered a loss, which is not a question under the Bankers Blanket Bond; and once the district court found that the Bank suffered a loss it held the Insurer liable without considering the language of the Bankers Blanket Bond as relevant to the issue of whether that loss was covered under the Bankers Blanket Bond.

5

To the reader's bewilderment, the writer has buried four cru-
cial points in one overburdened sentence. Here are the four
points:

- First, the court read only a part of the Bankers Blanket Bond.
- Second, the court read that part incorrectly.
- Third, and as a consequence, the court failed to focus on
  the proper issue in the case.
- Fourth, the dispositive issue in the case is whether the loss
  was covered under the Bond.

Each thought is central to the writer's argument and deserves
a separate expression. Here is a better version:

> The district court addressed only the term "realized" as used in
> the Bankers Blanket Bond. Then the court considered
> whether the appellee "realized" a benefit and the Bank suf-
> fered a loss. At that point, the court incorrectly held the In-
> surer liable. The issue is whether that loss was covered under
> the Bond.

Now the writer's argument is laid out clearly for the appellate
court. Remember that judges, like other readers, can assimilate
only limited amounts of information at one time. Present your
arguments in easily understood sentences, and you're more
likely to convince your judge.

Consider also that a clear, concise paragraph stating the issue
would necessarily appear early in the brief. There is an advan-
tage to be gained by impressing the court with effective writing
early in the document. Wisconsin Supreme Court Justice William A. Bablitch, a longtime advocate of better legal writing,
says: "When I see a good introductory paragraph, I dance."

⚖ Rule 2.   Use active voice verbs wherever appropriate.

Active voice verbs carry meaning with more vigor and exactness
than passive voice verbs. We're all familiar with government
press releases that exonerate officials by the use of the passive

voice: "Military aircraft were improperly used for personal travel."

An example from a lawyer's letter to a client also makes the point:

> The recommendation is made by our firm that the computation and crediting of interest be performed by the Accounting Department at the end of each fiscal year.

Although the meaning of the statement is relatively clear, consider the simplicity and directness of the active voice version:

> We recommend that the Accounting Department compute and credit interest at the end of each fiscal year.

To convert a passive voice verb into active voice, you simply name the doer of the action as the subject of the verb. In the example above, "our firm" is doing the recommending, so we recast the sentence to say "Our firm recommends" or "We recommend." We've also shortened the sentence by converting the long passive voice phrase "computation and crediting of interest be performed by the Accounting Department" into its active voice equivalent: "that the Accounting Department compute and credit interest."

Occasionally, you'll prefer not to say who did the action described, or perhaps you'll employ the passive voice to give variety to your sentence structure. But remember, the close connection between subject and verb in the active voice construction will add vigor and precision to your sentence.

◥ Rule 3.   Make verbs do the work in your sentences.

Often, writers use verbs plus nouns to express ideas rather than using the verb to directly express the underlying meaning. Take a look at this sentence:

      verb   **noun**
Please *provide* a *statement* of why you are interposing
     noun
an *objection* to the question.

Notice the concision of a short, succinct directive:

Please *state* your *objection* to the question.

Notice also how the emphasis on the vigorous word—the verb—places emphasis on action. The sentence below is weakened by the placement of the main idea in a noun instead of a verb:

verb   **noun**
It *is* my *recommendation* to you as regards the course of action you can probably pursue . . .

By making a verb out of the noun *recommendation*, we shorten the sentence and make it more forceful:

verb
I *recommend* the following course of action . . .

If we prefer a more tentative statement, we could recast the sentence with a different verb:

verb
You *might consider* the following course of action . . .

Although we've changed the meaning here, the verb is still doing the "work" in the sentence by carrying the main idea.

Verbs form the backbone of a sentence and carry the gist of the writer's expression. Our word *verb* comes from the Latin *verbum,* meaning *word.* So choose your most important words—verbs—carefully, and make them count.

⚖ Rule 4.   Remove surplus words.

Unfortunately, legal writers seem particularly susceptible to verbosity. Notice that although the sentence below is understandable, the important words are weakened by the frequent imposition of useless words and phrases.

> Our qualified experts place emphasis on the market's instability, and it is their careful and studied opinion that Atlanta's growth rate may decline in the event that the economy falters.

Trimmed up, this statement marches along on its useful words, and does not waste the reader's time or deflect the reader's attention with superfluous words.

> Our experts emphasize the market's instability, and they believe that Atlanta's growth rate may decline if the economy falters.

We've used the true verb here—"emphasize"—instead of the weak verb-plus-noun phrase "place emphasis."

The sentence is also strengthened by the deletion of "it is their careful and studied opinion," a tiresome and unconvincing commentary on the validity of the experts' opinion.

"In the event that" is another commonplace legal writing phrase that means nothing more than "if."

This typical legal wording was found in an explanation of insurance benefits:

> In the event that Joint Life Coverage has been selected by you . . .

In the revision, we've used "if" and converted the passive voice verb to the active voice. The phrase is now quite easily read:

> If you have selected Joint Life Coverage . . .

⚖ Rule 5.   Remove redundant legal phrases.

Legal writers have inherited a particular problem with redundancy. You may recall our discussion in the introduction to this book of Norman and Saxon "doublings" and "triplings." These redundancies persist in legal writing because writers often don't bother to discriminate between useful and useless words.

You may have seen contractual language similar to the following excerpt:

> First and foremost, the cosigner assumes all obligation and responsibility for any liability or loss arising under the terms of this agreement, and any act inconsistent with, or in violation of, this contract renders it null, void, and of no effect whatsoever.

A simpler version might read:

> The cosigner is liable for any loss under this agreement, and any act in violation of this contract nullifies it.

The second statement contains the legal substance of the first. Some legal writers, however, might be inclined to use the longer example simply because it does contain more words.

A better standard for the author's word choice would be the decision to use words that express different meanings instead of repetitive ones. For example, if you believe that the phrase "any act inconsistent with" adds something to the meaning of the sentence, you could revise in this manner:

> The cosigner is liable for any loss under this agreement, and any act inconsistent with, or in violation of, this contract nullifies it.

It is the author's prerogative to use words that express meaning best. The use of two or three words that express the same meaning, however, makes the reader think the writer has no precise meaning.

⚖ Rule 6.   Use everyday language whenever possible.

Although terms of art are essential to the profession, legal writers sometimes rely on useless, antiquated, or unclear phrases. This example is taken from an actual motion submitted to the court:

> The parties agree that this stipulation shall be submitted to the court for approval and adoption as an order of the court by issuance of the tendered form of order at the foot hereof.

What the writer means, and should have said, is that an order is attached. The words "by issuance of the tendered form of order at the foot hereof" are superfluous to the meaning of the document and are confusing to the reader.

Most legal documents have an intended audience of nonlawyers as well as legal professionals. Statutes, decisions, motions, orders, contracts, and almost any other legal writing you can think of (except perhaps legal memoranda) will be read by nonlawyers.

Nonlawyers may not know the Latin term *inter alia,* meaning "among other things," but legal writers often use such Latin terms to impress the reader rather than to express a meaning easily rendered in English. (For an extended discussion of law-yerisms and terms of art, see Rules 11 and 12.)

⚖ Rule 7.   Prefer specific and concrete words.

Although legal concepts and issues are necessarily abstract, legal writers often fall into the habit of writing or speaking entirely in abstract statements. These abstract statements rarely create a visual picture for the reader. They leave only vague impressions. Here is a fuzzy quotation from a lawyer in a newspaper interview:

> One of the things we're confronting in trying to increase understanding of the laws affecting the elderly is there is a lot of misunderstanding.

This lawyer obviously wants people to be better informed about laws involving the aged. She or he might have said:

> We run into a lot of misunderstanding about laws affecting the elderly.

A direct, simple statement would have improved the message—and the public's perception of lawyers.

Here's a vague statement from a law firm about its hiring practices:

> The firm has concurred with the efforts to augment its personnel recruitment parameters.

The precise meaning here is puzzling to the reader. Since the verb *to concur* suggests agreement, the reader is confused about why the firm would agree with its own efforts to do something. The word *augment* generally means *increase* or *enlarge,* and since it is combined with *parameters* we deduce that the firm is trying to recruit personnel in a new way.

Our version is more specific:

> The firm is actively recruiting from minority groups.

Occasionally, legal writers will choose to be purposefully vague. But if intentional obscurity is not your goal, remember to use precise words.

⚖ Rule 8.   Place modifers carefully.

In their search for accurate and unambiguous meaning, legal writers necessarily use extensive modification. Writers should not, however, let faulty modification ruin the meaning of a sentence. In the example below, ambiguous modification leaves open the main idea of the sentence.

> The Company's ownership percentage includes 700 shares or 2.9 percent of the Bank's outstanding shares which were issued as director's qualifying shares.

It's not clear whether the writer is referring to the 700 shares or to an alternative consisting of 2.9 percent of the Bank's outstanding shares. Additionally, as we read through the sentence, we see another ambiguity concerning the *which* clause. Normally, a *which* clause modifies the noun or pronoun just preceding the clause. But here the writer has given us more than one way to think about the *shares,* so we're confused.

A revision of the sentence clears up the ambiguities:

> The Company's ownership percentage includes 700 director's qualifying shares, which amount to 2.9 percent of the Bank's outstanding shares.

If you were drafting an agreement to purchase stock, the ambiguity of the first sentence might prove costly.

And if you are reading the following excerpt from a municipal ordinance, you might think you had discovered a loophole for "nonconforming activities":

> No substantial improvement affecting a wetland shall be made
> to an activity without a permit.

The introduction to this statutory section shows that the drafters
meant to prohibit certain activities. The revised version is more
precise:

> No substantial improvement affecting a wetland shall be made
> to a nonconforming activity.

⚖ Rule 9. Avoid placing too many subordinate clauses in one sentence.

Sentences may be so complex and indirect that the reader is
simply perplexed. The following sentence appeared in an appellate court decision:

> We are persuaded that the husband understandably would not
> know that the mere fact that the parties had cohabited before
> their formal marriage would later be made the basis of a
> theory that the parties had a common law marriage.

The presence of four subordinating conjunctions ("that") signals an unnecessarily complicated sentence. Rewritten, the sentence could be improved by omitting half of the conjunctions.

> We are persuaded that the husband would not know that co-
> habitation might amount to a common law marriage.

Compare the legal meaning of the two versions. Is anything
necessary to the judicial point missing from the second one?

⚖ Rule 10. Use conventional punctuation marks.

There are many rules of punctuation, but we have chosen to
emphasize, in this capsule review, three that are especially trou-
blesome for legal writers.

1. Use commas only where they are required. Legal writers, like
all careful writers, should recognize the difference between re-

strictive and nonrestrictive clauses. Restrictive clauses so define (restrict) the modified word that they are essential to the meaning of the sentence. Nonrestrictive clauses merely add additional information about the modified word and are not essential to the meaning of the sentence. Consider the "who" clause in the following example:

> Attorneys, who are required to take CLE courses, may claim as deductions all costs incurred in connection with legal writing seminars.

By enclosing the "who" clause in commas, the writer has indicated information that is merely additional and not essential to the main idea of the sentence. The logical meaning of the sentence, however, dictates that the commas be removed, allowing the clause to assume its rightful role of defining which attorneys may claim deductions.

2. Use a semicolon to separate two independent clauses not joined by a coordinating conjunction. The word *however* is often used in legal writing. But many writers are unsure about punctuating a compound sentence (a sentence containing two or more independent clauses) that has *however* between the two independent clauses. Take a look at this incorrectly punctuated sentence:

> The defendant hoped for a quick decision, however, the jury remained deadlocked after two weeks of deliberation.

If we change the sentence by deleting *however* and substituting a coordinating conjunction such as *but,* the comma between the two independent clauses is correct.

> The defendant hoped for a quick decision, but the jury remained deadlocked after two weeks of deliberation.

Alternatively, the sentence could be correctly punctuated with a semicolon before the *however.*

> The defendant hoped for a quick decision; however, the jury remained deadlocked after two weeks of deliberation.

3. *Be careful when using "it's."* Remember that *it's* means *it is* (or occasionally *it has*).

It's a wonderful life.
It's been a pleasure meeting you.

Writers often confuse the contraction *it's* with the possessive form of the pronoun *it*. The possessive form of the pronoun *it* has *no* apostrophe.

Each group will have its own legal assistant.

The apostrophe is not needed here because the pronoun *its* shows possession through its form.
The construction *its'* is always incorrect.

2

Principles of Diction

Diction refers to the choice and use of words in speaking and writing. Lawyers (and other legal writers) have a lexicon replete with both useful technical terms, called terms of art, and useless terms: jargon, redundancies, wordy phrases, and obsolete words. Unfortunately, these useless terms are at least partially responsible for the public perception of lawyers as windbags.

Take the following example of contractual language often presented as lawyers' entertainment. When an ordinary man gives an orange to another, he merely says, "I give you this orange." But when a lawyer does it, he says it this way:

> Know all men by these presents that I hereby give, grant, bargain, sell, release, convey, transfer, and quitclaim all my right, title, interest, benefit, and use whatever in, of, and concerning this chattel, otherwise known as an orange, or citrus-orantium, together with all the appurtenances thereto of skin, pulp, pip, rind, seeds, and juice, to have and to hold the said orange together with its skin, pulp, pip, rind, seeds, and juice for his own use and behoof, to himself and his heirs in fee simple forever, free from all liens, encumbrances, easements, limitations, restraints, or conditions whatsoever, any and all prior deeds, transfers, or other documents whatsoever, now or anywhere made to the contrary notwithstanding, with full power to bite, cut, suck, or otherwise eat the said orange or to give away the same, with or without its skin, pulp, pip, rind, seeds, or juice.

(For a longer version of this story told at a conference of the American Bankers' Association in 1976, see Carl Felsenfeld and Alan Siegel, *Writing Contracts in Plain English* [1981].)

You'll notice that strings of synonyms give bulk, and little else, to the paragraph above. Although historically it may have been prudent to use more than one word to say the same thing in more than one language, today's lawyer is rarely required to do so. Here are some handy rules to help you with diction.

⚖ Rule 11.   Use only essential words from traditional legal phrases.

As you read the following list, ask yourself if one word is sufficient for meaning, instead of two or three. You'll see that one word in each pairing is usually more familiar than the longer phrase and is quite precise by itself.

acknowledge and confess	acknowledge
act and deed	act
annul and set aside	annul
authorize and empower	authorize
conjecture and surmise	conjecture
covenant and agree	agree
cover, embrace, and include	include
deem and consider	consider
due and payable	due
each and all	each
each and every	each
entirely and completely	entirely
final and conclusive	final
fit and proper	proper
fit and suitable	suitable
for and during	during
for and in consideration of	for
force and effect	effect
fraud and deceit	fraud
free and unfettered	free

from and after	from
give and grant	give
give, devise, and bequeath	give
goods and chattels	goods
have and hold	have
heed and care	heed
hold and keep	hold
hold, perform, observe, fulfill, and keep	(choose the most suitable single word)
in lieu, in place, instead and in substitution of	instead of
in my stead and place	in my place
in truth and in fact	(choose either, depending upon the word you want to emphasize)
just and reasonable	reasonable
keep and maintain	maintain
let or hindrance	hindrance
lot, tract, or parcel of land	lot
made and provided	made
made, ordained, constituted, and appointed	(choose the most suitable single word)
maintenance and upkeep	maintenance
meet and just	just
mind and memory	mind
modified and changed	modified
null and void	void
of and concerning	concerning
ordered, adjudged, and decreed	ordered
over, above, and in addition to	in addition to
pardon and forgive	pardon
part and parcel	part
peace and quiet	peace
remise, release, and quitclaim	(choose the most suitable single word)
rest, residue, and remainder	remainder

revoked, annulled, and held for nought	revoked
save and except	except
seized and possessed	possessed
shun and avoid	avoid
situate, lying, and being in	lying in
stand, remain, and be	remain
truth and veracity	truth
void and of no effect	void
will and testament	will

No doubt you are familiar with most of these words and phrases, and perhaps it is this same familiarity that makes you hesitate to tamper with any of them. But the next time you're tempted to use any of these legal redundancies, think about what you are trying to say and use the one precise word that states your meaning.

⚖ Rule 12.   Avoid lawyerisms.

Lawyerisms are words and phrases used by lawyers but seldom used by anyone else. Unfortunately, lawyerisms give the appearance of precision, but they are rarely precise. Some of these legal terms still in use may have been appropriate in the past, but they are often merely anachronistic today.

To understand what is problematic about lawyerisms, we must first distinguish them from their legitimate cousins, terms of art. Terms of art are useful legal words that, over time, have come to refer to recognizable legal concepts. They may be Latin terms—*res ipsa loquitur*, for example—or they may be ordinary English words with a specialized meaning—*proximate cause*, *negligence*, and *foreseeability* are just a few.

Although there is no consensus among legal writing commentators about exactly which words are terms of art, they all agree that these technical terms have no exact synonyms, and that they operate as a kind of shorthand among lawyers. That means, of course, that you may on occasion find yourself using many words to explain these terms of art to nonlawyers. In fact, that's a test of a term of art. Terms of art are useful simply because they provide a "short" way to refer to a "long" concept.

Could you imagine yourself using many words to explain the legal concept behind *aforesaid*? Let this query guide you in choosing the right word or term: Does the word or term express precisely the meaning you want, and have you chosen the most economical language possible?

It's no accident that *aforesaid* is the archetypal example of a lawyerism. At first glance it may seem that *aforesaid* is a word indicating precision, as in "the aforesaid witness." If there is only one witness mentioned in the document, however, the word *aforesaid* is certainly superfluous. But what if there are many witnesses mentioned? Then "witness Smith" or "the witness for the defendant" will certainly be more precise and save the reader the trouble of rereading the document to locate the "aforesaid."

Here's a list of lawyerisms and some suggested substitutions.

above captioned	this case, this claim
aforementioned	(delete or rename)
aforesaid	(delete or rename)
attached hereto	attached is, attached are
during the course of	during
forswear	give up, renounce
forthwith	immediately
hereafter	from now on
hereby	(delete)
herein	in this document
hereinabove	the above
hereinafter	here called
hereof	of this
heretofore	previously
herewith	along with this
hitherto	up to now
in regard to	about, regarding
inasmuch as	since, because
in reference to	about, regarding
moreover	further, in addition
said (as an adjective)	(delete or replace with "the")

saith	says
same (as a noun)	(use appropriate pronoun)
thence	from that time, from that place
thenceforth	from then on
thereabout	nearby
thereafter	from then on
there at	there
therefor	for this, for that
therefrom	from it, from that
therein	in
thereof	(delete)
thereon	on
thereout	(delete)
thereover	(delete)
therethrough	(delete)
thereto	(delete)
theretofore	(delete)
thereunder	(delete)
therewith	(delete)
to wit	for example
whensoever	whenever
whereas	(delete unless you mean "on the contrary")
whereat	at what, at which
whereby	by which
wherefore	why, for what
wherein	in what, in which
whereof	of what, of which
whereon	on what
whereupon	after which
whilst	while
witnesseth	(delete)

You'll notice that the column on the left is reminiscent of bygone centuries, but the column on the right is made up of everyday words and phrases. Try to use everyday words in your writing unless you need a specifically technical word for precision of meaning.

⚖ Rule 13.   Use Latin and French terms only for firmly entrenched legal concepts.

Although you may be tempted to blame the preference for foreign words on the judiciary as a whole, note this practical advice found in the *Judicial Opinion Writing Manual* (American Bar Association, 1991):

> Avoid Latinisms and other foreign terms that are not necessary terms of art. Terms like "habeas corpus" and "voir dire" are indispensable to legal writing; "vel non" and "sub judice" are not. "Among other things" is understood by all; "inter alia" may not be.

Nonetheless, Judge Ruggero J. Aldisert expresses a common sentiment in his excellent *Opinion Writing* (1990). After reminding the reader of the maxim, "Avoid Latin expressions," he confesses, "Even so, I love them." His rationale? "They can be useful as shorthand substitutes for long rambling sentences."

Because the language of the law has inherited many Latin and Old French terms, you may also find yourself routinely using foreign words in legal documents and in court. Although we believe that foreign words should be used as little as possible to avoid burdening the reader with the necessity of translation, some foreign words are very useful for designating firmly entrenched legal concepts.

You may find yourself requesting a *guardian ad litem* for a minor child, or advising someone to get a *pro se* divorce. Or you may ask the court for *in personam* jurisdiction or, perhaps, *quasi in rem* jurisdiction. If you are drafting a will, you'll probably need to know if the client prefers *per stirpes* or *per capita* distribution of assets.

You might prepare an *amicus curiae* brief, defend a claim on the basis of *laches* or *estoppel*, or ask for dismissal on the ground of *res judicata*. If you do criminal defense work, you may need a writ of *habeas corpus*. And you've probably seen an order of the court marked *nunc pro tunc* to give it retroactivity.

Remember our earlier discussion of the "military accident" that led to the many French words in our legal vocabulary? Some of these words are still used. *Laches,* for example, is a term of art referring to an excessive delay in asserting a claim that may cause a court, as a matter of equity, to deny the claim.

Here are some additional Old French terms still used by legal writers: *cestui que trust, chose in action,* and *cy pres.* These three terms are readily translated: *beneficiary of a trust, a thing in action,* and *as near as possible* (to the testator's intention). These terms are often useful among lawyers and judges because they are both short and commonplace, at least in legal circles.

The longer the foreign phrase, however, the more difficulty for the reader. Unless you are well-schooled in Latin, you're going to have difficulty with this maxim: *In ambiguis casibus semper praesumitur pro rege.* You'll find this translation in *Black's Law Dictionary* (5th ed., 1979): "In doubtful cases the presumption is always in favor of the king."

You'll also need your *Black's* for this passage from an Illinois appellate decision: "Parens patriae cannot be ad fundandam jurisdictionem. The zoning question is res inter alios acta." This Roman mouthful recently won the dubious distinction of a Legaldegook Award from the State Bar of Texas.

Since almost all legal writing has an intended audience that includes nonlawyers, the Illinois Appellate Court might have simplified this passage in this manner: "Parens patriae cannot be made the basis of jurisdiction. The zoning question falls within the rule forbidding the introduction of collateral facts."

Perhaps our translation isn't exactly what the Illinois court meant. This imprecision is precisely the problem with over-reliance on foreign words: they are always subject to translation. The court could have said what it meant more directly in English.

3

Principles of Tone

Tone, in writing, means the writer's attitude toward the reader, the subject matter, or a combination of the two. You, as writer, are able to control the tone you use to get the result you want. Your tone will be as varied as the writing you do. A demand letter will have a very assertive tone. A brief to the court will contain a persuasive tone, and a letter to your client will usually reflect a friendly, yet professional tone.

Since law is by its nature an adversarial business, lawyers get used to being assertive and aggressive. These are useful attributes for the courtroom and for pursuing a settlement or negotiation. But when assertion and aggression appear on paper, they often take the form of insult. Almost every law student learns to avoid the argument against the person and to prefer the argument against the issue.

⚖ Rule 14.   Don't insult the reader.

Sometimes the writer's language works against the desired result, as in these actual examples:

> *Poor:* No one could conscientiously contend that . . .
> *Better:* Our contention is . . . *or,* We disagree with your contention . . .
> *Poor:* There are some factors that you don't seem aware of.
> *Better:* There are some additional factors that you may wish to consider.

25

The desired result here is, of course, to get the reader to read and consider the writer's point of view, not to cause hostility or annoyance.

You may remember searching for the appropriate tone in your first appearances in court. You quickly learned the appropriate terms of respect: "May it please the court," for example. These familiar and useful terms of address are an essential part of the formal, ritualized court setting. Often, however, finding the "right" tone in pleadings, motions, and briefs is difficult because you, the advocate, must find a way to be persuasive without overstating your position or challenging the court's authority.

In the following example, the writer (Appellant Insurer's counsel) comes dangerously close to implying that the court doesn't have sense enough to differentiate fact from fiction.

> Appellant Insurer's counsel, in working on this brief, appreciate the difficulty in maintaining fiction separate from truth. . . . We relay a caveat in such regard to the court.

There is no "good" version of this caveat to the court. It's the writer's job to persuade the court, not to warn it about possible misinterpretation. Such a patronizing tone does nothing to advance the writer's argument and is certain to annoy the judge whose intelligence is questioned.

⚖ Rule 15. Don't waste the reader's time.

Much legal writing is meant to be persuasive. In addition to clarity and accuracy, an appropriate use of tone will help the writer convince the reader. Consider how this sentence from a lawyer's motion for a continuance wastes the court's time:

> *Poor:* I am embarking upon an emergency departure from the State of Colorado this present day and respectfully request the court to temporarily excuse my presence.
> *Better:* Please excuse my temporary absence from the state because of a family emergency.

The improved example is polite, specific, and concise. Surely the court will also be convinced that the writer is a person who does not waste words or the court's time.

Here is another example from the appellate brief discussed in Rule 14. It's clear from this next example that the writer is having a difficult time getting to the point, and as a consequence, the reader is distracted by this useless preamble:

> Parenthetically, this Insurer would tend to disagree that . . .

There's no improved version of this example, either. The word "parenthetically" is a sure sign that the reader should prepare for volubility. In order to be convincing, the writer must agree or disagree. A tendency to agree or disagree is merely annoying to the reader you're trying to persuade.

🔨 Rule 16.   Avoid legal jargon.

In Rule 12, we made a distinction between useful legal words, terms of art, and useless words, lawyerisms. There is another category of useless legal words and phrases, which we call *legal jargon.* These terms are close cousins to lawyerisms, but you wouldn't be tempted to designate any of these phrases terms of art. In fact many of these wasteful words have found their way from legal writing into business writing, especially when the writer mistakes a pompous or overbearing attitude for an assertion of authority.

Here's a list of often-used terms that can either be eliminated entirely or translated into more useful language.

> *And/or:* Avoid this construction unless you're asking a question. (It's sometimes useful in interrogatories when you'd like to open up the answer.) In a declarative sentence, it often indicates ambiguity. If *and* and *or* alone won't do the job, try this construction, "X or Y or both." Precision in wording makes for a convincing tone.
>
> *Comes now the plaintiff:* An antiquated beginning for a complaint, this phrase is modernized by using more natural word

order: "Plaintiff Mary Doe, by her attorneys Walton & Williams, states . . ."

For the purpose(s) of: This phrase is just a long-winded version of *for* or *under.* "For the purposes of section 46, a beneficiary shall mean . . ." And "Under section 46, a beneficiary shall mean . . ." Do you see any difference in meaning in these two examples?

Further affiant (deponent) saith not: Since these words say nothing useful, and give your writing a distinctive sixteenth-century flavor, leave them out.

In lieu of: Here's a Latinism that has a perfectly good English equivalent, *instead of.* Use English terms instead of foreign terms whenever possible. Your readers will appreciate your directness.

The fact that: While it's true that lawyers often argue over the "facts," you should avoid this wordy phrase unless you are making a specific assertion about a fact. Notice how the phrase is unnecessary in this example: "Because of the fact that the law requires a unity of interest created at the same time by the same instrument . . ." Removing the useless phrase serves to focus the reader on the legal concepts. "Because the law requires a unity of interest created at the same time by the same instrument . . ."

With respect to: Avoid the imprecision of this wordy phrase and choose another word or rewrite your sentence.

⚖ Rule 17.   Avoid "provided that" if possible.

Irving Younger described this term as "odious," and with good reason. Writers employing this term play a trick on the reader by giving and taking away in the same sentence. See if you can readily unravel the meaning of this sentence taken from a credit insurance application:

> The Disability Policy provides, if you become totally disabled commencing while insured for this benefit with respect to your loan and you continue to be totally disabled for more than the number of days shown in the application, we agree to pay periodically to the Credit Union one monthly disability

> benefit stated herein for each month of your continued total disability, beginning with the day benefits commence as shown in the application, provided, however, that no benefit shall be payable for any period of your continued total disability after the original maturity date of your loan or after death.

Obviously, this sentence is far too long to be comprehensible. The *provided, however, that* structure led the writer down the primrose path of sentence overload. The revised version is broken into three sentences, with the proviso given emphasis in a separate sentence.

> If you become totally disabled while insured for this benefit, and you continue to be totally disabled for more than the number of days shown on this application, we agree to pay periodic benefits to the Credit Union. These monthly disability benefits will be paid each month of your continued total disability, beginning with the day benefits commence as shown in this application. However, no benefit shall be payable for any period of your continued total disability after the original maturity date of your loan or after death.

By removing the *provided that* phrase, we were able to give the reader two declaratory statements and then signal the qualifying statement very simply with the word *however*.

Although *provided that* is still pervasive in statutory language, you'll find your writing is more easily understood if you avoid using this phrase.

⚖ Rule 18. Avoid sexist language.

Gary Blake and Robert W. Bly, in *The Elements of Business Writing* (1991), note that "over the past twenty-five years, the world of business has grown sensitive to the problem of sexist terms. . . . Now that women make up more than half the work force, it is no longer accurate—or fair—to use terms that once were taken for granted." This advice should not be ignored by legal professionals for the same pragmatic reason: women are now an increasing presence in every aspect of the working world.

Lawyers who specialize in the field of labor and employment law are advising their clients to avoid using language that is restricted solely to the male gender. Now, for example, an old, taken-for-granted term like *workmen's compensation* is commonly called *workers' compensation*. An employee handbook written solely with the masculine pronoun would give the appearance, at least, of an employer who considers only the masculine half of the work force.

All legal writers should become aware of sexist terms in order to avoid offending clients or attracting allegations of gender bias. The ABA's *Judicial Opinion Writing Manual* formulates this rule: "When possible, use gender-neutral terms."

But avoiding sexist language often presents some problems for us, as writers, as we try to maintain both grammatical correctness and gender-neutral language. Some masculine nouns are difficult to convert to neutral terms: for example, conman, craftsman, and draftsman are not improved by these changes: conperson, craftsperson, and draftsperson. Other masculine nouns have more neutral-sounding alternatives: fireman, policeman, and businessman become firefighter, police officer, and manager (or retailer or entrepreneur).

To avoid gender bias when using pronouns, you may need to vary your writing style. Here are some suggestions for replacing the masculine pronoun (unless of course you are referring to a specific male).

Rewrite to eliminate the pronoun.

> *Poor:* If a lawyer wishes to sound unbiased, he must . . .
> *Better:* Lawyers who wish to sound unbiased must . . .

Repeat the noun.

> *Better:* If a lawyer wishes to sound unbiased, the lawyer must . . .

Make the antecedent noun a plural.

> *Better:* Lawyers who wish to sound unbiased must . . .
> *Better:* If lawyers wish to sound unbiased, they must . . .

Use the second person pronoun.

Better: If you wish to sound unbiased, you must . . .

Although the rules of language use do change over time, it's still considered grammatically incorrect to use this construction: "If a lawyer wishes to sound unbiased, they must . . ." In this example, the pronoun *they* is plural, but the antecedent noun *lawyer* is singular. The grammatically correct choice would be somewhat unwieldy "If a lawyer wishes to sound unbiased, he or she (she or he?) must . . ." This pronoun pair is occasionally useful, as well as correct, but it becomes tedious by constant repetition. You may wish to try some of the forms suggested above to avoid constantly repeating the pronoun pair.

You're probably familiar with this standard legal language: "The masculine pronoun includes the feminine . . . wherever appropriate."

Although this statement may be an economical way to avoid repetition of pronoun pairs, it may indicate a lack of sensitivity to gender issues. Writers should always consider the particular purpose and audience for the writing when choosing pronouns.

◣ Rule 19.   Don't use "Dear Sir" unless it fits the reader.

If you're still using the salutation "Dear Sir" without giving much thought to the prospective reader, consider this response from a law firm we know. Letters addressed to the firm with the accompanying salutation "Dear Sir" receive this reply:

> I received the enclosed letter from you in the mail this past week. I am returning it to you since there must have been some mistake in sending it to me. Since the salutation reads "Dear Sir," I am certain this was only intended for male attorneys. Some of us are not.

Since "Dear Sir or Madam" is outdated, you might use a generic term when you do not know the gender of the reader. Try, for example, "Dear Attorney," or "Dear Office Manager," or some other appropriate title for the reader.

4

Principles of Grammar

The sentence is the basic grammatical unit. Although we don't always speak in complete sentences, written communication is usually expressed in sentences.

A sentence is a group of words that expresses a complete thought by means of a *subject* and a *predicate*.

The *subject* is that part of a sentence about which something is asserted. The subject is the naming part of the sentence, in which the writer identifies what she or he is telling us about.

> *She* testified.
> *The zealous advocate* was untiring.
> *The witness with the hoarse voice* made a noise like that of a foghorn.

The complete subject includes all the words that name or describe what is being talked about.

However, the simple subject (a noun or pronoun) is essential for grammatical analysis. Here are the simple subjects found in the preceding examples:

> *She* testified.
> The zealous *advocate* was untiring.
> The *witness* with the hoarse voice made a noise like that of a foghorn.

The *predicate* is that part of a sentence which says something about the subject. The predicate provides an explanation of the action, condition, or effect of the subject.

He *lied on the witness stand.*
The defendant *waived her right to a speedy trial.*
The witness *fainted when his prior testimony was revealed.*

The complete predicate contains all the words that make a statement about the subject. The simple predicate, however, contains only the important word or words in the assertion: the verb. Note the important words—the verbs—in the above examples: *lied, waived,* and *fainted.*

In this chapter, we'll identify the parts of speech and the principles guiding their correct use. The eight parts of speech are *nouns, pronouns, adjectives, adverbs, verbs, prepositions, conjunctions,* and *interjections.*

Nouns

A noun is a word used to name a person, place, thing, or condition.

person: parent, wife, Judge Rosetti
place: Wyoming, Puget Sound, Boston
thing: desk, monument, pistol
condition: pandemonium, honesty, goodness

Nouns are also classified as common or proper. A *common* noun signifies one of a class:

city, woman, office

A *proper* noun is a special name given to individualize a person, place, or thing. Proper nouns are always capitalized:

Seattle, Eleanor Roosevelt, Empire State Building

Nouns may have many different functions.
As the subject of a sentence:

The *desk* is dusty again.

As the object of a verb:

The hunter shot the *tiger* after it attacked the *child.*

As the predicate nominative (noun):

This *book* is a *classic*.

As the subject of an infinitive (the unconjugated form of a verb, which is always preceded by *to*):

The judge asked the *witness* to leave the room.

As the object of a preposition:

The lawyer dropped his pencil on the *floor*.

As the indirect object:

She gave her *dog* a bone.

As a word denoting possession:

The bailiff returned to the *judge's* chambers.

As a word of direct address:

Officer, arrest that man.

As an appositive (noun following another noun and further describing it):

Professor Keen, our *instructor*, is very dull.

As the modifer before another noun.

The *silver* candelabrum was tarnished.

As the modifier of a verb.

He left *yesterday*.

Collective Nouns

When a common or proper noun signifies a group, it is called a *collective noun*. A collective noun may be either singular or plural. Some examples of collective nouns are *mob*, *jury*, *Congress*, and *committee*.

⚖ **Rule 20. When a collective noun is thought of as a single unit with all the individuals of the group acting together, use a singular verb.**

The jury *has* reached a verdict.
The committee *is* unanimous in its approval of the bill.

⚖ **Rule 21. When a collective noun is used in such a way that the individual members of a group are thought of as acting separately, use a plural verb.**

The jury *have* different opinions on the question of her guilt or innocence.
The committee *are* unable to agree on the location of the meeting.

Compound Nouns: Forming Plurals

Compound nouns are nouns composed of more than one word. There are special rules governing plural forms of many of these compounds.

⚖ **Rule 22. Form the plural on the principal word of a compound noun separated by a preposition.**

attorney-at-law	attorneys-at-law
mother-in-law	mothers-in-law
power of attorney	powers of attorney

⚖ **Rule 23. Form the plural on the noun in a phrase consisting of a noun followed by an adjective.**

heir apparent	heirs apparent
knight-errant	knights-errant

If the principal word of a noun compound is the second word, form the plural there.

vice president   vice presidents
trade union   trade unions

Possessive Before Gerund

⚖ **Rule 24.   Form the possessive case of a noun or pronoun immediately preceding a gerund.**

A gerund is a verb form (verbal) ending in "ing" and used as a noun. In the example below *resigning* is the gerund form of the verb *to resign,* so the noun or pronoun preceding the gerund must be in the possessive case.

Mary's resigning would be disruptive to the firm.

Note, however, that personal pronouns have unique possessive forms that do *not* use the apostrophe:

Her resigning would be disruptive to the firm.

Pronouns

A pronoun is a word that is used instead of a noun. Pronouns may be classified as follows:

A *personal pronoun* is one that shows by its form whether it represents the person speaking (first person), the person spoken to (second person), or the person, place, or thing spoken of (third person):

Singular	*Plural*
First person: I, my, mine, me	we, our, ours, us
Second person: you, your, yours	you, your, yours
Third person: he, his, him	they, their, theirs, them
she, her, hers, it, its	

A *relative pronoun* introduces a clause and not only refers to some noun or pronoun as its antecedent but also connects the clause in which it stands with that antecedent:

> This is a court *that* clears its docket.
> He is the witness *whom* you examined.
> Show him the agreement *that* you drew.
> The agreement, *which* has been signed by the parties, is now being challenged.

An *interrogative pronoun* is used in asking a question:

> *Who* is walking to the courthouse?
> *Which* attorney did you consult?
> *What* is his alibi?

A *demonstrative pronoun* is used to take the place of something that is pointed out with particularity:

> Which report do you prefer? I prefer *this*.
> Will you take these sheets? No, I will take *those*.

An *indefinite pronoun* refers to unspecified persons or objects:

> *Everyone* is presumed innocent.
> *Any* and *all* can sit in judgment.
> *Each* must decide for himself or herself.

A *possessive pronoun* refers to an antecedent that possesses a person or thing and may stand alone:

> The law journal is *his*.
> *Theirs* is the burden of choosing personnel.
> *Mine* is the duty of sifting the evidence.

A *reflexive pronoun* redirects the action of the verb to the subject:

> He showed *himself*.
> We must strengthen *ourselves*.

An *intensive pronoun* is used to give emphasis:

He will ride the horse *himself*.
She *herself* was not injured.

⚖ Rule 25.   Use reflexive pronouns only to redirect the action of the verb to the subject or for emphasis.

Wrong: Please call Marge O'Brien or *myself* if you need more information.

Right: Please call Marge O'Brien or *me* if you need more information.

Wrong: The committee met with William Martinez and *myself*.

Right: The committee met with William Martinez and *me*.

Pronoun Cases

Pronouns, like nouns, have three cases (categories): *nominative*, *possessive*, and *objective*.

The *nominative* case is found where the pronoun is used as a subject or predicate nominative.

The *possessive* case is used to show ownership.

The *objective* case is found where the pronoun functions as a direct object, indirect object, or object of a preposition.

The following chart illustrates the various forms of the personal pronouns:

Nominative		Objective		Possessive	
Singular	*Plural*	*Singular*	*Plural*	*Singular*	*Plural*
1st person					
I	We	Me	Us	My	Our

Nominative		**Objective**		**Possessive**	
Singular	*Plural*	*Singular*	*Plural*	*Singular*	*Plural*
2nd person					
You	You	You	You	Your	Your
				Yours	Yours
3rd person					
				His	
He		Him		Her	Their
She	They	Her	Them	Hers	Theirs
It		It		Its	

Pronouns must agree with their antecedents in person, number, and gender, but not in case. The case of pronouns is determined by their function within the sentence.

Nominative case:

> *She* excused the witness. (*She* is the subject of the sentence.)
> The witness is *he*. (*He* is the predicate nominative.)

Possessive case:

> This brief is *hers*. (*Hers* shows possession.)
> *Her* brief is concise. (*Her* shows possession.)

Objective case:

> The judge excused *him*. (*Him* is the direct object of the verb.)
> The officer read *him* his rights. (*Him* is the indirect object of the verb.)
> The officer put the handcuffs on *him*. (*Him* is the object of the preposition *on*.)

Indefinite Pronouns

We often have difficulty with indefinite pronouns because they do not have antecedents to guide us in determining verb agreement.

There are, however, a few simple rules about indefinite pronouns worth remembering.

⚖ Rule 26. Most indefinite pronouns require a singular verb.

Indefinite pronouns that require a singular verb include *each, either, neither, somebody, nobody, everybody, anyone,* and *nothing.*

> *Each* of us must do *his* own work.
> *Each* of us must do *her* own work.
> *Each* of us must do *his* or *her* own work.

The use of a plural pronoun when referring to a singular subject is always incorrect.

> *Wrong: Each* of us must do *their* own work.

⚖ Rule 27. Those indefinite pronouns referring to more than one person or thing take plural verbs.

Such indefinite pronouns include *several, few, both,* and *many.*

> *Several* of us *think* otherwise.
> *Few care* about the matter.

⚖ Rule 28. Like collective nouns, some indefinite pronouns may be either singular or plural depending on whether they refer to a singular or plural concept.

Indefinite pronouns that may be either singular or plural include *some, any, none, all,* and *most.*
 When one of these ambiguous pronouns is the subject of the sentence, and a prepositional phrase follows the pronoun, the prepositional phrase will indicate either a singular or plural idea.

None of the estimates *are* accurate.
None of the material *is* appropriate.

When there is no prepositional phrase following the indefinite pronoun, you may choose either a singular or a plural verb to show your intended meaning. Usually, however, the context surrounding the sentence will be helpful.

None *are* accurate. (the estimates)
None *is* appropriate. (the material)

When there is no expressed antecedent, the pronoun *it* will function as an indefinite pronoun. When *it* begins a sentence, *it* should be considered singular even though it may seem to refer to a predicate that is plural.

It is the parents who must suffer the consequences.

Relative Pronouns

The following rules will help you to choose the correct relative pronoun: *who, whoever, whom,* and *whomever;* and *which* and *whichever.*

⚖ Rule 29.   Use "who" and "whoever" when referring to persons and when the nominative case is required.

She is the reporter *who* gave us the information. (*Who* is the subject of the verb *gave*.)
Give the application to *whoever* shows up. (*Whoever* is the subject of the verb *shows*. The *–ever* ending indicates the pronoun means *anyone that*.)

⚖ Rule 30.   Use "whom" and "whomever" when referring to persons and when the objective case is required.

Although *whom* and *whomever* are rarely used in speech, careful writers still observe the rules requiring the objective case for pronouns.

It was she *whom* they selected for the position. (*Whom* functions as the direct object of the verb *selected*.)

We shall send the certificates to *whomever* you prefer. (*Whomever* functions as the direct object of the verb *prefer*, and the meaning is *anyone that* you prefer.)

⚖ Rule 31.   Use "which" and "whichever" when referring to animals or objects.

The *dog*, which was kept outside, barked all night long.
You may choose chocolate or vanilla, *whichever* you prefer.

See Rule 76 for a discussion of the use of *that* or *which* to introduce restrictive and nonrestrictive clauses.

Adjectives

Adjectives describe or limit nouns or pronouns.
Predicate adjectives complete the meaning of a verb:

The weather was *stormy*.
The coffee tastes *bitter*.

Many adjectives are found immediately preceding the noun they modify:

Stormy weather is great for ducks.

Adjectives have an attribute called *degree*. The three degrees are the *positive*, the *comparative*, and the *superlative*.

⚖ Rule 32.   The positive degree indicates a quality of an object.

The issues are great and the record is *small*.
The lawyer is *erudite*.

⚖ Rule 33.   The comparative degree indicates that the qualities of two objects are being compared.

The issues are *greater* and the record *smaller* in this case than they are in the former case.
Her lawyer is *more erudite* than his.
Wrong: She was the smartest of the two partners.
Right: She was the smarter of the two partners.

⚖ Rule 34.   The superlative degree indicates that the qualities of three or more objects are being compared.

The issues here are *the greatest* and the record *the smallest* that I have ever encountered.
Her lawyer is *the most erudite* of all in this county.

Avoid forms of the comparative or superlative adjective that are not recognized by correct usage:

Wrong: She was the *beautifulest* dancer in the chorus line.
Right: She was the *most beautiful* dancer in the chorus line.

A few adjectives are compared irregularly:

Positive	Comparative	Superlative
bad	worse	worst
good	better	best
little	less	least
much	more	most

⚖ Rule 35.   When two or more nouns are in apposition (describing further the preceding noun), the article is placed only before the first.

Articles are the little adjectives *a, an,* and *the.*

He received a letter from Mr. Roe, *the* attorney and counselor at law.

⚖ Rule 36. When "this," "these," "that," and "those" are used as adjectives, they must agree in number with the modified noun.

Wrong: These kind of clients.
Right: That kind of client.
Right: Those sorts of seeds.

⚖ Rule 37. Do not use the comparative or the superlative degree of adjectives that already express absolute qualities.

Wrong: It has a *most universal* appeal.
Right: It has a *universal* appeal.
Wrong: That drug is the *fatalest* one at all times.
Right: That drug is *fatal* at all times.
Wrong: This is the *most unique* case on today's docket.
Right: This case on today's docket is *unique*.
Right: This *unique* case is on today's docket.

In all formal writing and speaking, comparisons should be completed. Words that clarify or complete comparisons must not be omitted:

Wrong: She is the most ungrateful client.
Right: She is the most ungrateful client *I've ever had*.
Wrong: This seminar is more enjoyable.
Right: This seminar is more enjoyable *than the one we attended last month*.
Wrong: He liked the judge better than his mother.
Right: He liked the judge better *than his mother did*.
Wrong: The grip of a gorilla is many times more powerful than a man.
Right: The grip of a gorilla is many times more powerful *than a man's* (or *than that of a man*).

Adverbs

An *adverb* is a word that modifies a verb, an adjective, or another adverb. Adverbs answer questions about place, time, manner, degree, and to what extent:

Place (where?):

> The hearing was held *there*.

Time (when?):

> We expect relief *soon*.

Manner (how?):

> He stopped *quickly*.

Degree (how much?):

> She handled the case *entirely* on her own.

To what extent:

> The door opened *wide*.

There are some adverbs that, like adjectives, can be compared in three degrees: the positive, the comparative, and the superlative:

The positive degree:

> Ben types *rapidly*.
> Mary runs *fast*.

The comparative degree:

> Ben types *less rapidly* than Ned.
> Mary runs *faster* than Ann.

The superlative degree:

> Ben types the *least rapidly* of all the men.
> Mary runs the *fastest* of all the runners.

⚖ Rule 38. Use an adverb to modify a verb or an adjective, but do not use an adjective to modify a verb.

Wrong: I *sure* don't want to miss it.
Right: I *surely* don't want to miss it.
Wrong: He speaks *real* well.
Right: He speaks *very* well.
Wrong: They could do this work *easy*.
Right: They could do this work *easily*.
Wrong: You can haul this *easier* with a cart.
Right: You can haul this *more easily* with a cart.

Verbs

A verb is a word or group of words that asserts action, condition, or state of being.

The client *signs*.
He *is*.
The property *stands* vacant.

Rarely will a sentence have only a subject and a verb. Most sentences contain words in the predicate that either complete the action of the verb or further describe the subject.

These verb completers may be readily identified once you have determined what kind of verb you have. All verbs fall into two main categories: *action* or *linking*.

Verb Completers

Action verbs do just what the term implies. They describe, sometimes in a very general way, physical activities. Some activities are easy to identify: *run, throw, strike*. Other action verbs require some imagination: *decline, have, plead*.

Some action verbs:

The hail *pelted* the windows.
The ocean *roared*.

Linking verbs (sometimes called copulative verbs) demonstrate a very close grammatical relationship between subject and verb. All forms of the verb *to be* are linking verbs, as are many verbs of the senses.

Some linking verbs:

> They *are* attorneys.
> She *seems* tired.
> The clerk *sounded* angry.
> I *am* hungry.
> She *is* the loser.
> The pen *was* on the desk.
> They *were* our clients.
> I *feel* good (or bad).

Action verbs have two kinds of completers: *direct objects* and *indirect objects*.

Direct objects. To find the direct object, ask the question *What?* or *Whom?* about the verb. The direct object indicates the recipient of the action of a transitive verb.

> The judge admonished the *witness*.
> She declined his *invitation*.

Indirect objects. Finding indirect objects is easy if you remember that they are *always* located between the verb and the direct object in the sentence. The indirect object usually tells to whom or for whom the action of the verb is done.

> The settlement check brought *us* welcome relief.
> He gave the *witness* a difficult time.

Linking Verbs also have two kinds of completers: *predicate adjectives* and *predicate nominatives*.

Predicate adjectives. Look for an adjective (descriptive word) that completes the linking verb by describing the subject.

> She was *precocious*.
> The bailiff was *angry*.

Predicate nominatives. Look for a noun or pronoun that completes the linking verb by restating the subject.

Your waiter is *Georgio*.

Rule 39. In formal writing, use the nominative case of the pronoun following a linking verb.

The perpetrator is *he*.
The speaker is *she*.

An understanding of verb completers will be especially useful for you in choosing the appropriate form of the pronoun. Remember that pronouns undergo a change in form (also called *case*) depending upon their function in the sentence.

Pronouns that complete the action of *action verbs* are in the objective case:

She warned *him*. (*Him* is the direct object and is in the objective case.)
He gave *her* the brief. (*Her* is the indirect object and is also in the objective case.)

Subject-Verb Agreement

In addition to understanding verb completers, you may wish to review rules governing subject-verb agreement. Some of the more important rules follow.

Rule 40. Compound subjects connected by "and" take a plural verb unless the subjects are identical in person or thing, or are so closely related as to be singular in idea.

Heredity and *environment are* both contributory factors.
The *house* and the *garage have been destroyed* by the fire.
The *father* and *guardian* of this boy *is* guilty of gross negligence. (*Father* and *guardian* refer to the same person.)
The *rod* and *reel was* useless. (The subject is being used in a singular sense.)

⚖ Rule 41.   Where a noun intervenes between the subject and its verb, it must not interfere with the agreement of subject and verb, even though the intervening noun may be different in number from the subject.

The *briefcase,* as well as the contracts and the bonds and mortgages, *was found* in the bus.
The *pearls* on the tray *have retained* their luster.
The *treasurer,* in company with all of the members of the board, *is* downstairs in the lounge.
His *team,* together with all the teams in the league, has to abide by the rules.

⚖ Rule 42.   When the elements of a compound subject are connected with the correlative conjunctions "either . . . or," or "neither . . . nor," the subject is considered singular if all the elements are singular, and plural if all the elements are plural.

Either the *pens* or the *pencils are* to be returned.
Neither *she* nor *he walks* rapidly.

⚖ Rule 43.   When one of the elements of a compound subject is plural and the other is singular, and the elements are connected with the correlative conjunctions "either . . . or," or "neither . . . nor," the number of the verb is governed by the element closer to the verb.

Neither the *teacher* nor the *pupils are* at fault.
Either the *pupils* or the *teacher is* at fault.

A noun that is plural in form but singular in use usually takes a singular verb:

The *ethics* of the profession *is* of great importance.
Measles is a disease of short duration.
Politics is sometimes a dirty business.

Rule 44. A verb with a collective noun as its subject is singular if the noun represents a unit, but plural if the noun is thought of in its individual parts.

The *jury* was unanimous in its verdict.
The *jury were* divided on the question of his guilt.
The *squad was* a tightly knit unit.
The *squad were* given diverse assignments.

Rule 45. A relative pronoun having a plural antecedent (noun to which the pronoun refers) must have a plural verb.

Wrong: He is one of those *optimists who is* never crestfallen.
Right: He is one of those *optimists who are* never crestfallen.

In the example above, the word *optimists* is the antecedent of the relative pronoun *who.* If the sentence were changed so that *one* is the antecedent of *who,* then the verb would be singular:

He is *one who is* never crestfallen.

Shall and Will

The distinction between *shall* and *will* is still observed in formal writing, but in informal usage *will* is employed for all three persons.

Rule 46. To express simple futurity, use "shall" in the first person and "will" in the second or third.

I *shall* stay there all week.
You *will* be delighted to meet him.
She *will* notify you when he arrives.

Rule 47.   To express promise, determination, choice, intention, command, or threat, use "will" in the first person and "shall" in the second and third persons.

I *will* pay this bill next week. (promise)
We *will* not give up. (determination)
I *will* choose that one. (choice)
I *will* proceed as I see fit. (intention)
You *shall* carry out every order. (command)
He *shall* suffer for such conduct. (threat)

Active and Passive Voice

Verbs are found to be in either the *active voice* or the *passive voice* depending upon whether the subject of the verb does or receives the action of the verb.

The active voice should generally be preferred because the active voice is more forceful than the passive voice. (See Rule 2.)

Active voice: The marine *fired* his rifle six times.
Passive voice: The rifle *was fired* by the marine six times.
Active voice: He *typed* the brief in a day.
Passive voice: The brief *was typed* by him in a day.

Rule 48.   Use the passive voice for stylistic variety, or when it's not important for the reader to know who did the action of the verb.

When you wish to stress a person or a thing that receives the action, or when the particular person or the thing which does the acting is not definitely known, use the passive voice.

The rifle *was fired* and the prisoner halted.
The brief *was typed* on a word processor.
The garment *was torn* to shreds.
The passengers *are directed* to their seats.

Occasionally, however, a shift in voice achieves a significant purpose:

Active: As the horsemen *ascended* the slope . . .
Passive: . . . they *were cheered* by a bedraggled group of men.

Here, the shift in voice is justified because it keeps the attention focused upon the horsemen; the subject in both clauses is kept within the reader's range of attention.

Mood

Mood is the inflectional change of a verb to indicate the manner in which an action or state is expressed.

The *indicative mood* is used chiefly in statements of fact and in questions:

He *enjoys* singing.
Have you *lost* your wallet?

The *imperative mood* is used in commands and requests:

Close the door after you leave.
Help us with our work.

The *subjunctive mood* is used to express a condition contrary to fact (after *if* or *as though*) or to express a wish. Such uses occur principally in written English and usually apply to only one verb form—*were*.

Rule 49. Use "were" to indicate the subjunctive mood.

Contrary to fact:

If I were [not *was*] you, I'd learn to speak well. (I am not you.)
If he *were* [not *was*] stronger, he'd be an athlete. (He is not stronger.)

Wish:

I wish it *were* [not *was*] true.
She wishes that she *were* [not *was*] leaving town next week.

Tense

Tense indicates the power of the verb to show differences of time. There are six tenses in common use.

The *present tense* represents an action that occurs, or a condition that exists, at the present time:

> I *play.*
> She *dances.*
> He *turns* red.

The *past tense* represents an action that occurred, or a condition that existed, at some past time:

> I *played.*
> She *danced.*
> He *turned* red.

The *future tense* represents an action that will occur, or a condition that will exist, at some future time:

> I *shall play.*
> She *will dance.*
> He *will turn* red.

The *present perfect tense* represents an action that is complete, or a condition that has already come to pass, at the time of utterance:

> I *have played.* She *has danced.* He *has turned* red.

The *past perfect tense* represents an action that was completed, or a condition that had come to pass, at some time in the past:

> I *had played.*
> She *had danced.*
> He *had turned* red.

The *future perfect tense* represents an action that will be completed, or a condition that will have come to pass, at some time in the future:

I *shall have played.*
She *will have danced.*
He *will have turned* red.

There are certain basic rules about using tenses that will make for smooth and effective writing. The most important rule is:

⚖ Rule 50.   Avoid unnecessary shifts in the tense of verbs.

At the conference, the Governor *reads* a lengthy letter but *refuses* to make any comments. (Both verbs are present tense.)
At the conference, the Governor *read* a lengthy letter but *refused* to make any comments. (Both verbs are past tense.)

Generally, the tense of the verb in a dependent clause should be the same as the tense of the verb in the main clause:

Portia *did* not *attend* the conference because she *was* ill. (Both verbs are past tense.)
Henry *prefers* chess because it *stimulates* his thinking. (Both verbs are present tense.)

But, to express a universal truth, use a past tense in the main clause followed by a present tense in the subordinate clause:

She *believed* that hard work *is* rewarded.

⚖ Rule 51.   If necessary, use a split infinitive for precision of meaning.

An infinitive is a tenseless form of the verb preceded by *to: to be, to do, to see.* Although some grammatical purists avoid placing an adverb between the *to* and the root verb, most writers choose precision of meaning over rigid adherence to antiquated rules.

The President of the United States, for example, promises "to *faithfully* execute" the duties of the position. Notice the slight but awkward difference in meaning of a promise *to execute faithfully* or *faithfully to execute*.

Prepositions

A *preposition* is a word joined to a noun or pronoun to show its relation to the other words in the sentence:

> He crawled *under* the wagon wheel.
> She waited *at* the stage door.
> They walked *through* the front entrance.

A *prepositional phrase* contains a preposition and its object and may be used as either an adjective or an adverbial modifier, and occasionally as a noun.

Adjectival modifier:

> A lawyer *from his district* spoke. (Adjectival modifier of *lawyer*)

Adverbial modifier:

> She practices law *from September to June.* (Adverbial modifier of *practices*)

Noun:

> *From nine to five* is the usual time to work. (Noun, subject of the verb *is*)

Although prepositions are usually found at the beginning of a phrase, they often fall correctly and naturally at the end of a sentence. This idiomatic use of prepositions is an important aspect of English style.

⚖ Rule 52.   Do not hesitate to place a preposition at the end of a sentence when naturalness and common use dictate.

> He is the man I argued *with*.
> These are the ideas that we agreed *upon*.

At the moment, that is all I can think *of.*
What kind of vehicle was she traveling *in?*

Conjunctions

A *conjunction* is a word used to join words, phrases, clauses, or sentences. In addition to the conventionally recognized conjunctions—*coordinating, subordinating,* and *correlative*—we will also take a look at *conjunctive adverbs.*

A *coordinating conjunction* is used to connect expressions of equal rank:

The meat was juicy *and* tender.
I knocked *but* no one answered.
Have you spoken to Dick *or* Doris?

There are seven common coordinating conjunctions. They're easy to remember in the form of the acronym FANBOYS: *for, and, nor, but, or, yet,* and sometimes *so.* (Note that *however* is not a coordinating conjunction. See Rule 53 for more advice about punctuating compound sentences.)

The FANBOYS conjunctions are used to join independent clauses with a comma preceding the conjunction.

I researched the case, *but* I was unable to find any useful information.

A *subordinating conjunction* is one that connects a dependent clause with a main clause:

When you have completed the project, notify me.
Please call him *before* you leave.
Although the speaker was boring, we listened.

Correlative conjunctions are used in pairs to join sentence elements of equal rank:

Either you go, *or* I go.
Neither coffee *nor* tea suited his taste.
If speech is silver, *then* silence is gold.

Rule 53. Always use a colon or semicolon between the independent clauses in a compound sentence when a conjunctive adverb links the clauses.

A *conjunctive adverb* is one that is used to connect independent clauses:

> She was disturbed with the conversation; *thus,* she left the room.
> He wanted a Rolls Royce; *however,* he settled for a Cadillac.

Other conjunctive adverbs are *therefore, hence, moreover, also, thus, then, still, accordingly, consequently, furthermore, likewise, nevertheless,* and *besides.*

Interjections

An *interjection* is a word or exclamatory sound that expresses emotion or feeling and has no grammatical relation to the sentence in which it is found.

Examples of interjections are *Oh! Hurray! Hush! Ouch! Damn! My goodness!*

Rule 54. Use an exclamation mark to punctuate interjections.

> Bravo!
> Aha!
> Objection!

5

Principles of Syntax

The term *syntax* refers to the pattern of word order in a sentence. Well-constructed sentences should reveal *unity, coherence,* and *emphasis*.

Unity

⚖ Rule 55. A sentence must display oneness of thought in order to be comprehensible to the reader.

> *Poor:* As she finished her summation to the jury, she realized that she had failed to stress an extremely vital point, and so she motioned to co-counsel seated at the plaintiff's table and then on the way out of the courtroom, she stopped to speak to her client.

Although each clause has the same grammatical subject, the sentence as a whole is not a unit because it combines ideas that are not closely related.

> *Better:* As she finished her summation to the jury, she realized that she had failed to stress an extremely vital point. She motioned to co-counsel seated at the plaintiff's table. Then, on the way out of the courtroom, she stopped to speak to her client.

Unrelated ideas in a sentence destroy the rule of unity. In the three separate sentences of this revised example, related ideas are pulled together and readability is improved.

Sentences also transgress the rule of unity if they state too little.

> *Poor:* Martine rode to the Federal Courts Building with her attorney. Having met him at the corner of Main and Broadway.

"Having met him at the corner of Main and Broadway" is a sentence fragment: It makes no sense without the preceding independent clause.

> *Better:* Martine rode to the Federal Courts Building with her attorney, having met him at the corner of Main and Broadway.

Although writers sometimes use coordinating conjunctions to begin sentences, those conjunctions normally show a close relationship between elements of a compound sentence.

> *Poor:* The witness was not properly prepared this morning. But, she will be prepared in the afternoon session.
> *Better:* The witness was not properly prepared this morning, but she will be prepared in the afternoon session.

Even when related ideas are grouped together in a sentence, the relationship should be clearly shown by the use of *connectives* and *punctuation*.

⚖ Rule 56.   The independent clauses in a compound sentence must be separated by either a comma followed by a coordinating conjunction or a major punctuation mark (colon or semicolon).

> *Poor:* The firm was pleased that he won the case, he worked hard and mastered every aspect of litigation.
> *Better:* The firm was pleased that he won the case, for he worked hard and mastered every aspect of litigation.
> *Better:* The firm was pleased that he won the case; he worked hard and mastered every aspect of litigation.

Coherence

In any well-constructed sentence, the proper relationship of words should be unmistakably clear.

⚖ Rule 57.   To avoid misreading, place modifying words next to words they modify.

Words such as *nearly, not,* and *only* should be placed close to the modified word. Note the change in meaning that results from different word placement in these examples:

> She sold *nearly* a thousand shares.
> She *nearly* sold a thousand shares.
> All pit bulls are *not* vicious.
> *Not* all pit bulls are vicious.
> *Only* he saw her smile to him.
> He *only* saw her smile to him.
> He saw *only* her smile to him.
> He saw her *only* smile to him.
> He saw her smile to him *only*.

⚖ Rule 58.   Clauses beginning with relative pronouns (that, which, who, whose, whom) should be placed close to the modified word.

> *Poor:* Elizabeth carried a rough draft of the agreement in her briefcase, which she handed to her client.
> *Better:* In her briefcase, Elizabeth carried a rough draft of the agreement, which she handed to her client.

A phrase or clause may be so carelessly placed in a sentence that it is ambiguous.

> *Poor:* The lawyer, notwithstanding his incarceration, told the accused to trust the legal system.
> *Better:* The lawyer told the accused to trust the legal system notwithstanding his incarceration.
> *Better:* The lawyer told the accused, notwithstanding his incarceration, to trust the legal system.

⚖ Rule 59.   Introductory modifying phrases and clauses must have a logical relation to the modified word.

Poor:

Checking carefully, an error was discovered. (indicates that the error did the careful checking)

After seeing her dentist, her teeth stopped aching. (indicates that her teeth saw the dentist)

Drinking heavily every night, his reputation suffered. (indicates that his reputation was doing the heavy drinking)

Sentences that illustrate coherence contain the introductory modifying phrase that can logically modify the pronoun or noun that follows.

Better:

Checking carefully, her secretary discovered the error.

Her teeth stopped aching after she saw her dentist.

Because he drank heavily every night, his reputation suffered.

Pronouns without a definite referent are confusing to the reader.

Poor: We may attend the trial, for *she* is my sister's friend.

Better: We may attend the trial, for the defendant is my sister's friend.

Pronouns that may refer to two (or more) antecedents are ambiguous.

Poor: The lawyer told the client that *his* son was driving *his* car.

Better: The lawyer said to the client, "Your son was driving your car."

Coherence is also violated when grammatical constructions *after* coordinating conjunctions differ in form from the construction *before* the conjunction.

Poor: That is a perfect example, and which I admonish you to follow.

Better: That is a perfect example, which I admonish you to follow.

Better: That is a perfect example, and I admonish you to follow it.

Emphasis

Emphasis, as it applies to sentence structure, means an arrangement of words that gives distinction to the main ideas and subordinates the less important details.

Rule 60. To emphasize important words, place them at either the beginning or end of the sentence.

The emphatic places in a sentence or clause are the *beginning* and the *end*.

Poor: Many a woman has devoted her life to an important cause, *it is worthy of note.*

Better: Many a woman, *it is worthy of note,* has devoted her life to an important cause.

By shifting the relatively unimportant clause "it is worthy of note" to an unemphatic position in the middle of the sentence, we improve the force of the sentence.

We may also emphasize certain words by placing them out of their natural order in the sentence.

Everywhere they encountered the same indifference.
Great is the power of knowledge.

Emphasis may be shown by *contrast* or *antithesis.*

To err is human; to forgive, divine.
I judge by actions, not mere words.

A sentence may be made emphatic by arranging ideas in *order of importance.*

An arrangement of words, phrases, and clauses in *order of importance* often makes a sentence emphatic by causing a continual heightening of interest.

Poor: His reputation, his automobile, his life, his friends, his social position, were all at stake.

Better: His automobile, his social position, his reputation, his friends, his life itself, were all at stake.

⚖ Rule 61.   Emphasize important ideas by subordinating less important ideas in dependent clauses.

Careful writers direct the reader's attention by placing less important ideas in dependent clauses. The independent clause thus carries—and emphasizes—the main idea.

Poor: Her bus was late, and she missed her appointment.

Better: Because her bus was late, she missed her appointment.

Poor: When Lincoln wrote his famous address, he was riding through the woods.

Better: While riding through the woods, Lincoln wrote his famous address.

Using the active voice of a verb often provides *emphasis* because the active voice verb is stronger in tone than the passive voice. In the active voice, the subject of the verb does the action of the verb. (See Rule 2.)

Active voice: My attorney rejected your offer.

Passive voice: Your offer was rejected by my attorney.

⚖ Rule 62.   Avoid repetition.

Emphasis is often gained by economy in words. Avoid redundancies and tautologies.

A *redundancy* is a grammatical repetition.

Poor: I shall never repeat *again* the experience of my first trial.
(*again* is superfluous)

Better: I shall never repeat the experience of my first trial.

A *tautology* is a repetition of same idea.

Poor: There was a complete silence, and not a sound could be heard.

Better: There was a complete silence.

Sometimes, though, we gain emphasis by repeating important words.

... and that government of the *people*, by the *people*, and for the *people*, shall not perish from the earth.

Faults in Sentence Structure

Period Fault

A *period fault* occurs when a sentence fragment is punctuated as if it were a complete sentence. Sentence fragments can usually be corrected by either (1) incorporating the fragment into the sentence of which it is logically a part, or (2) expanding the fragment into a complete sentence.

Poor: The mediator kept on trying in the face of difficulties. Hoping she would ultimately find a solution to the problem.

Better: The mediator kept on trying in the face of difficulties, hoping she would ultimately find a solution to the problem.

Better: The mediator kept on trying in the face of difficulties. She hoped that she would ultimately find a solution to the problem.

Sentence Fragments

⚖ Rule 63. Avoid writing sentence fragments.

Phrases and subordinate clauses should not be written as complete sentences, because they do not express a complete thought.

Phrases:

Poor: Charles had a noble trait. To speak well of all people.

Better: Charles had a noble trait: to speak well of all people.

Better: Charles had a noble trait; he spoke well of all people.

Subordinate clauses:

Poor: Judy said that she had never practiced law. Though she was licensed to practice in two states.

Better: Judy said that she had never practiced law, though she was licensed to practice in two states.

Better: Judy said that she had never practiced law. However, she was licensed to practice in two states.

Appositives are nouns that follow other nouns and further describe them.

Appositives should not be used as complete sentences.

Poor: His briefcase contained a variety of documents. Namely, contracts, leases, affidavits, and releases.

Better: His briefcase contained a variety of documents: namely, contracts, leases, affidavits, and releases.

Comma Faults

A *comma fault* occurs when the writer places a comma between two independent clauses. This error can be corrected by (1) eliminating the comma and writing the two independent clauses as separate sentences; (2) inserting a coordinating conjunction (*for, and, nor, but, or, yet, so*) after the comma; (3) substituting a semicolon for the comma; (4) subordinating one of the sentences to the other; or (5) reducing one of the sentences to a phrase.

Poor:
The lawyer had not won a single case all year, she was dejected.

Better:

Separating sentences: The lawyer had not won a single case all year. She was dejected.

Inserting a coordinating conjunction: The lawyer had not won a single case all year, and she was dejected.

Substituting a semicolon: The lawyer had not won a single case all year; she was dejected.

Subordinating a sentence: Since she had not won a single case all year, the lawyer was dejected.

Reducing a sentence to a phrase: Not having won a single case all year, the lawyer was dejected.

6

Principles of Punctuation

Punctuation, like other aspects of writing, changes with custom. The older, or "closed," system of punctuation is characterized by many commas. It is more formal than the newer, "open" system. The modern approach is to omit punctuation marks unless they are required by a rule. A good example of the two styles is the use of commas in a series of words.

If a sentence contains several words or ideas expressed in a series, the comma between the *and* and the last word or phrase can be deleted unless to do so would result in misunderstanding. Consider this illustration: "The law firm specialized in real estate, antitrust, personal injury and workers' compensation law." For clarity, you might place a comma after "personal injury" to emphasize that it is a field distinct from "workers' compensation."

As a matter of practice, punctuation styles may vary depending upon the particular publication. Harry Shaw, author of *Punctuate It Right!*, makes this observation about punctuation: "It is often illogical; common sense will not always be your salvation; certain punctuation practices are a matter of convention, nothing else." If you are drafting briefs, appeals, and other court documents, you may prefer the formal convention of "closed" punctuation. In letters to clients, newsletters, and magazine articles, you may choose the less formal "open" system.

The principles of punctuation dealt with in this chapter will give you an overview of the most common kinds of punctuation and some of the problem areas associated with them. For more information, consult the "Recommended Sources."

Periods

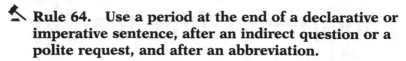

Rule 64.   Use a period at the end of a declarative or imperative sentence, after an indirect question or a polite request, and after an abbreviation.

Declarative sentence: The law is often ambiguous.
Imperative sentence: Speak clearly, please.
Indirect question: She asked the client if he wished to accept the settlement.
Polite request: May I have your attention.
After an abbreviation: Dr., Esq., Mr., Ms., etc., i.e., e.g.

Question Marks

Rule 65.   Use a question mark at the end of a direct question, after each of the elements of a series to provide emphasis, and in parentheses to indicate doubt.

After a direct question: Are you ready to testify?
To emphasize elements of a series of questions: What happened to the file? Where's the menu? The floppy disk? The print-out?
To indicate doubt: The trial took place in 1901 (?) in Idaho.

Never use a question mark after an indirect question.

I asked him if he was ready to testify.

Exclamation Points

Rule 66.   Use an exclamation point at the end of a complete or incomplete sentence to show strong emotion or intense feeling.

Strong emotion: How dare you contradict me!
Intense feeling: I will not give up!

Exclamation points should *not* be used to indicate emphasis.

Commas

Commas should never be placed randomly in a sentence and should not be used to repair an overly long sentence.

⚒ Rule 67. Use commas to separate words, phrases, and clauses in a series.

Words in a series: The practice was limited to wills, estates, and taxation.

Phrases in a series: He believed in the dignity of man, in the dignity of labor, and in the dignity of service.

Clauses in a series: The lawyer who communicates well with clients, who files timely motions, and who maintains good financial records reduces her risk of malpractice.

Note: Most legal writers prefer to keep the serial comma before *and* because they feel it's safer to do so, and because their readers expect to see the comma there. However, many writers (and some editors) routinely omit the comma before *and* in a series of words unless the omission would cause a misreading.

The practice was limited to wills, estates and taxation.

Although there is little chance of misreading the sentence above, legal writers usually insert the comma before *and*.

⚒ Rule 68. Commas are used between parts of geographical names, addresses, and dates.

Geographical names: The climate in Leadville, Colorado, is invigorating.

Addresses: 10 Downing Street, London, England

Dates: On Wednesday, July 4, 1990, he left for a vacation in New Zealand.

When the complete date is not given, commas may be omitted:

> She joined the firm in July 1990.

⚖ Rule 69.   Use a comma before a coordinating conjunction joining two independent clauses.

Coordinating conjunctions include *for, and, nor, but, or, yet,* and sometimes *so*.

> The defendant wept during the cross-examination, *but* the jury remained impassive.

If the sentence is short, and the meaning is clear without punctuation, the comma is often omitted before the coordinating conjunction.

> It rained *and* it snowed.

⚖ Rule 70.   Use a comma to prevent misreading.

> While we were eating, the dogs escaped.
> The day after, the rain reduced the fire danger.

Note: The test for misreading is applied at the place of ambiguity (eating the dogs? after the rain?), *not* at the end of the sentence. Readers should not have to reread a sentence to discover the meaning.

⚖ Rule 71.   Use a comma to separate introductory clauses and phrases from the rest of the sentence.

> Since the company refused to settle, we instructed our attorneys to sue.
> During the recess, the parties reached an agreement.

⚖ Rule 72.   Enclose parenthetical (added or interjected information) phrases with commas.

His work, having been done under stress, was worthless.
Her failure to report the incident, it seems, may weaken her testimony.

⚖ Rule 73.   Use a comma to set off words of direct address.

Bailiff, remove that man.
Ms. Jones, please help this woman.
May I ask for an interpreter, Judge Golden?

⚖ Rule 74.   Use a comma to enclose an appositive.

Appositives are nouns that directly follow other nouns and further describe them.

Marion Howes, president of our county bar association, was appointed to the bench.
We selected our new associate, William Mendoza, for the award.

⚖ Rule 75.   Use a comma to set off direct quotations.

The judge said, "Be seated, please."

But do not use a comma before the *that* introducing an indirect quotation.

The lawyer said that the trial would not last more than three hours.

⚖ Rule 76.   Use commas to enclose nonrestrictive clauses.

Nonrestrictive clauses are nondefining. They merely add information.

The problem of finding the heirs, which had now become quite
urgent, was brought to the court's attention.

Restrictive clauses are defining. They are essential to the
meaning of the sentence.

The man who attacked me is present in the courtroom.
The exhibit that proves my argument is quite complicated.

Lawyers often argue about the use of *which* or *that* to introduce a restrictive clause. Modern usage allows either one, according to *The Merriam-Webster Dictionary of English Usage*
(1989): "You can use either *which* or *that* to introduce a restrictive clause—the grounds for your choice should be stylistic—
and *which* to introduce a nonrestrictive clause."

Other style manuals and some editors take a different approach and recommend that the introductory *which* be limited
to nonrestrictive clauses.

Semicolons

The semicolon shows a greater degree of separation than a
comma shows.

⚖ Rule 77.   Use a semicolon between independent clauses not joined by one of the coordinating conjunctions (for, and, nor, but, or, yet and sometimes so).

Members of the judicial committee will attend the annual conference; it is scheduled to last five days.

⚖ Rule 78.   Use a semicolon between independent clauses joined by conjunctive adverbs.

Some common conjunctive adverbs are *for example, for instance,
that is, accordingly, besides, furthermore, therefore, nevertheless,
however, otherwise, hence, thus, still, instead, also, consequently.*

Counsel on both sides indulged in heated argument during the trial; nevertheless, the judge remained calm.

We rescind the contract; consequently, we no longer have an obligation to perform.

⚖ Rule 79.   Use a semicolon between independent clauses if there are many commas within the clauses.

The *Barrister*, a new legal journal, and one of the most original to appear in the past decade, advertised for an editorial cartoonist; and the applicants who responded, interestingly enough, were attorneys.

⚖ Rule 80.   Use a semicolon between elements of a series if there are commas within the series.

The following legal educators were elected to the interdisciplinary committee: Jeanette Dawson, dean of Valley Law School; Richard Riley, dean of Balfour Law School; and Gordon Grant, dean of Packard Law School.

Colons

The colon is often used as an introductory symbol.

⚖ Rule 81.   Use a colon to introduce formal statements.

At the pretrial conference you will have to decide the following: first, whether you ought to concede; and second, what your concession ought to be.

⚖ Rule 82.   Use a colon to introduce long quotations.

In his retirement speech, Justice Samson spoke as follows: "Looking back over my fifty years of law practice I have seen many changes . . ."

⚖ Rule 83.   Use a colon to introduce an independent clause that summarizes or particularizes the thought in the preceding clause.

A referee must possess one basic qualification: she must be fair.

⚖ Rule 84.   Use a colon to introduce a series of words, phrases, or clauses that itemize or specify what has been stated in the preceding clause.

The bylaws of the corporation provided for the following committees: executive, finance, and legal.

The state had openings in the following three departments: the tax department, the insurance department, and the auditing department.

The attorney advanced the following arguments in favor of retaining Mr. Dale: he was competent, he was loyal, and he was reliable.

⚖ Rule 85.   Place a colon after "the following," and "as follows."

(However, the colon comes before *namely, specifically,* and *for example.*)

The only jurors present were the following: Winken, Blinken, and Nod.

Announce the names as follows: Blinken, Nod, and Winken.

She had only one answer: namely, to try harder.

The child had many fine qualities: for example, he was always cheerful.

Colons should not be placed to separate a verb from its object or a linking verb from its completer.

Poor: To make lime punch you need: lime juice, sugar, water, and ice.

Better: To make lime punch you need lime juice, sugar, water, and ice.

Poor: The metals he was testing were: gold, silver, and copper.
Better: The metals he was testing were gold, silver, and copper.

Parentheses

Parentheses are used to enclose explanatory words, phrases, or clauses usually having no grammatical dependence on the rest of the sentence.

⚖ Rule 86.   Use parentheses to enclose material that is explanatory and loosely related to the rest of the sentence.

Georgina West (she was a born leader) was asked to become president of the new corporation.

At the close of our conversation, the attorney agreed to represent us (just as I predicted).

⚖ Rule 87.   Use parentheses to enclose material that confirms something written immediately before it.

Under a trust agreement, his son was to receive six hundred dollars ($600) a month.

You have thirty (30) days to submit your written objectives.

Brackets

Brackets are traditionally used to enclose certain types of explanatory material.

⚖ Rule 88.   Use brackets to show the addition of editorial comment to quoted matter.

"He gave no reason for his [the president's] sudden departure."
The witness said, "She [the defendant] refused to listen."

Rule 89.   Use brackets around the Latin word *sic*— meaning "thus it is"—to point out an error in quoted material.

"The waver [sic] was valid."
"Weather [sic] he wins is unimportant."

Rule 90.   Use brackets to enclose parentheses within a parentheses:

These statutes were printed in London (Poe and Poe [now Poe Ltd.]) in 1819.

Rule 91.   In formal writing, use brackets to show you've changed a capital letter to lowercase or vice-versa.

Also, "[a]bsent constitutional infirmity, it is not within the judicial power to exclude from a statute that which the legislature expressly includes."

Dashes

The dash is used to denote an interruption or sudden break in thought. It is a more informal mark of punctuation than a colon or a comma and should not be overused.

Rule 92.   Use a dash to denote a sudden break in thought.

We may—and according to plan, should—bring in additional counsel.
The summation—if, indeed, it could be called a summation—was a mishmash of confusion.

Rule 93.   Use a dash to mean "namely," "that is," "in other words," and similar expressions that precede explanations or elaborations.

The judge had the power to prevent the altercation—she could have stopped the trial at will.

The colon and dash are generally interchangeable as a mark of punctuation between two independent clauses, but remember that the colon is to be preferred in formal writing.

The judge had the power to prevent the altercation: she could have stopped the trial at will.

Rule 94.   Use a dash to enclose parenthetical material containing commas.

His future—which, as you are well aware, was our primary concern—did not seem to worry her one bit.

Rule 95.   Use a dash to precede a final summarizing clause in sentences having several elements as subject of the main clause.

Aldwin, who was a master of commercial law; Barstow, who was a master of litigation; and Caldwell, who was a master of appellate procedure—these were the original partners of the firm.

Rule 96.   Use a dash to show an addition or insertion that defines or enumerates a preceding word or phrase.

These items—paper, pencil, and eraser—were her only tools.
We are now approaching another part of town—the business district.

Apostrophes

Apostrophes are used to show possession, to denote omitted words or letters, and to form the plural of letters, figures, signs, or symbols.

⚖ Rule 97.   Use an apostrophe to show possession.

Singular nouns: Add an apostrophe *and* an *s* to singular nouns:

man's, woman's, boy's, girl's, attorney's, child's

If the singular noun ends in *s*, the added *s* is often omitted:

Mr. Jones' lawyer was generous.

However, some editors and writers prefer to keep the apostrophe plus *s:*

Dickens's criticism of the legal profession is often satirical.

Plural nouns: Add an apostrophe *and* an *s* to plural nouns not ending in *s:*

men's, women's, children's, geese's, alumni's

Add an apostrophe *after* the *s* to plural nouns ending in *s:*

brothers', sisters', girls', boys', attorneys'

Joint and separate possession: When two persons possess something jointly, use the apostrophe after the last noun only:

Winston and Barton's article is brilliant.

When two persons own something separately, use the apostrophe with each name:

Judy's and Robert's doors were open.

Compound nouns: Use an apostrophe *and* an *s* after the last word of a compound noun or pronoun:

my brother-in-law's problem
my brothers-in-law's problems

each other's problems
somebody else's problem

⚖ Rule 98.   Use an apostrophe in a contraction where a letter or letters are omitted.

He doesn't [does not] care.
It's [it is] snowing.
I'm [I am] through.
They're [they are] coming.

⚖ Rule 99.   Use an apostrophe to form the plural of a letter, figure, sign, or symbol.

There are four S's and two P's in Mississippi.
Her 7's look like 9's.
Tell him to put $'s before each figure.

Punctuated abbreviations also have an apostrophe following.

M.B.A.'s
J.D.'s

But unpunctuated abbreviations often have just an "s" to indicate the plural.

PCs
CLEs

Hyphens

Hyphens are often used in spelling compound words. Unfortunately, their use in compound words varies so greatly that no rule will cover all possibilities.

Since our language is constantly changing, you should consult a dictionary or recent edition of a grammar handbook for advice on writing compound words. See the general writing and reference books in the "Recommended Sources."

⚖ Rule 100.   Use a hyphen between the elements of familiar compounds.

brother-in-law
mother-in-law
sister-in-law
father-in-law
fellow-citizen
cross-examination

⚖ Rule 101.   Use a hyphen to avoid doubling a vowel.

anti-imperialistic
semi-invalid
ego-oriented

⚖ Rule 102.   Use a hyphen between words of an improvised compound.

a never-say-die attitude
a snake-in-the-grass conclusion
a drop-in-the-bucket response

Quotation Marks

Quotation marks are used to enclose a direct quotation, to indicate unusual (and often ironic) usage, and to call attention to certain kinds of titles.

⚖ Rule 103.   Use quotation marks to enclose direct quotations.

Counsel said, "Your Honor, I move for a directed verdict."
The judge said, "Motion denied."

Rule 104. Use quotation marks to indicate unusual or ironic usage of a word.

The partner advised the new associate that weekend work was "optional."

Rule 105. Use quotation marks to set off chapter headings and titles of articles, short stories, short poems, and works of art.

The article from the *ABA Journal* was entitled "Tort Reform: Nuisance or Necessity?"
"Poem in October" is a well-known poem by Dylan Thomas.

Rule 106. Use single quotation marks to enclose material quoted within a quotation.

The judge wrinkled her brow and answered, "Lincoln said, 'A lawyer's time and advice is his stock in trade.' "

Rule 107. Commas and periods should always be placed inside end quotation marks .

"Counsel may proceed," said the magistrate.
She believed him when he said "Honesty is the best policy."

Rule 108. Colons and semicolons should always be placed outside the end quotation marks.

This is the quintessence of the "Law of Torts": so exercise your rights as not to interfere with the rights of others.
In response to counsel's question, the witness stated, "I do not know"; then he asked to be excused.

Note: British publications usually place commas and periods outside the end quotation marks.

⚖ Rule 109.   Place question marks and exclamation points inside the quotation marks if they apply to the quoted matter.

"Are you listening?" she asked.
The captain managed to say, "We will never surrender!" before
   he collapsed on the deck.

⚖ Rule 110.   Place question marks outside the quotation marks if the question applies to the sentence as a whole.

Where can I find the quotation, "To err is human"?
Why did she say "Please leave me alone"?

7

Principles of Capitalization

There is much confusion concerning the use of capital letters. The best general guideline to follow is this: use capitals only for a specific purpose and in accordance with accepted principles.

For a comprehensive listing of rules of capitalization, consult the *U.S. Government Printing Office Style Manual,* Chapters 3 and 4. Here is a representative list.

⚖ Rule 111. Capitalize the first word of a sentence or a direct quotation.

The judge asked, "And how do you know?"
"No," the witness answered. "I have never seen the defendant before today."

⚖ Rule 112. Capitalize the first word following a colon if it begins a complete sentence and expresses a completely different thought from that preceding the mark of punctuation.

The issue is critical: Plaintiff's contention that the statute of limitations does not apply here is erroneous.

Note: Do not capitalize the first word following a colon when it introduces a closely related explanatory element.

We are never deceived: we deceive ourselves.

⚖ Rule 113.   Capitalize the first word in each complete sentence in an enumerated series preceded by a colon.

Her grounds for the motion were two: (1) The trial court refused to admit proper evidence. (2) The trial court abused its discretion in refusing to award attorney fees.

⚖ Rule 114.   Capitalize proper names and derivatives of those names.

Paris   Parisian
Italy   Italian

Derivatives of proper names that have acquired independent common meaning are not capitalized.

plaster of paris
italicize

⚖ Rule 115.   Capitalize a common noun or adjective forming an essential part of a proper noun.

Amazon River
Great Lakes
Larimer County
Central City
City of Aurora

Do not capitalize a common noun used alone to stand for the proper noun:

the river (Amazon)
the lakes (Great Lakes)
the county (Larimer County)
the city (Central City, City of Aurora)

Do capitalize a common noun used alone as a *well-recognized* short form of a proper noun:

the Capitol (Washington, D.C.), *but* the capitol (state)
the Channel (English Channel)
the District (District of Columbia)

⟍ Rule 116. Capitalize the full names of organized bodies and their shortened names.

National bodies:

Bureau of the Census, the Bureau
Department of Agriculture, the Department
Interstate Commerce Commission, the Commission
U.S. Supreme Court, the Court
U.S. Navy, the Navy

International bodies:

International Monetary Conference, the Monetary Conference,
   the Conference
Permanent Court of Arbitration, the Court
United Nations, the Council, the Assembly

⟍ Rule 117. Capitalize titles of cabinet members and other important officials.

President
Secretary of Transportation
Ambassador at Large
Governor
Lieutenant Governor

⟍ Rule 118. Capitalize the names of specifically named courts.

United States Supreme Court
Supreme Court of Illinois
Court of Appeals for the Tenth Circuit
District Court of El Paso County
Probate Court of Los Angeles County

Do not capitalize when a partial name is given or the reference is to courts in general.

> federal court
> state court
> district court
> trial court

The shortened form of the United States Supreme Court is *always* capitalized: the Court.

◣ Rule 119.   Capitalize words referring to specific persons, officials, groups, and government bodies.

> the Secretary of Transportation
> the Secretary
> the NLRB
> the Board
> the Environmental Protection Agency
> the Agency
> a Republican
> a Representative (U.S. Congress)

◣ Rule 120.   Capitalize such titles as chief justice, presiding justice, justice, judge, presiding judge, reporter, and clerk only when used with a person's name.

> Chief Justice Romero
> Presiding Justice Smith
> Mr. Justice Brennan
> Judge Sandstone
> Reporter Davis
> County Clerk Bell

Do not capitalize these titles when used alone.

> a judge of the Superior Court of San Joaquin County
> the reporter of the United States Supreme Court
> the county clerk

⚖ Rule 121. Capitalize titles of specific acts, laws, treaties, and similar documents.

Uniform Commercial Code
Declaration of Independence
Magna Carta
Treaty of Versailles
Colorado Court Rules

Do not capitalize unofficial or generic names of statutes, acts, and laws:

statute of limitations
revenue act
bankruptcy laws
code (unspecified)

The names of bodies of laws, rules, and regulations should be capitalized:

Laws of Delaware
California Rules of Civil Procedure
Treasury Regulations

⚖ Rule 122. Capitalize the names of civil holidays, historic events, and religious holidays.

Labor Day
Martin Luther King Day
Christmas
Battle of Bull Run
World War II
Feast of Tabernacles
Yom Kippur

8

Principles of Paragraph Construction

Paragraphs are groups of related sentences. The *paragraph* is one of the most important organizing units for legal writing. Since paragraphs reveal groupings of like ideas, you may wish to use these three factors to check the effectiveness of your paragraphs: *unity, coherence,* and *emphasis.*

Unity requires that all of the sentences within a paragraph bear directly on the main thought.

⚖ Rule 123. Construct all paragraph sentences around the main thought.

Notice how all the sentences in this paragraph from Price Waterhouse v. Hopkins, 490 U.S. 228, 232-33 (1989), give details about the topic sentence.

> At Price Waterhouse, a nationwide professional accounting partnership, a senior manager becomes a candidate for partnership when the partners in her local office submit her name as a candidate. All of the other partners in the firm are then invited to submit written comments on each candidate—either on a "long" or a "short" form, depending on the partner's degree of exposure to the candidate. Not every partner in the firm submits comments on every candidate. After reviewing the comments and interviewing the partners who submitted them, the firm's Admissions Committee makes a recommendation to the Policy Board. This

recommendation will be either that the firm accept the candidate for partnership, put her application on "hold," or deny her the promotion outright. The Policy Board then decides whether to submit the candidate's name to the entire partnership for a vote, to "hold" her candidacy, or to reject her. The recommendation of the Admissions Committee, and the decision of the Policy Board, are not controlled by fixed guidelines: a certain number of positive comments from partners will not guarantee a candidate's admission to the partnership, nor will a specific quantity of negative comments necessarily defeat her application. Price Waterhouse places no limit on the number of persons whom it will admit to the partnership in any given year.

Coherence means that the sentences in a well-constructed paragraph form a smooth chain of properly related thoughts.

⚖ Rule 124.   Write paragraph sentences to form a chain of related thoughts.

Concluding that James Joyce's famous novel is not pornographic, Judge Woolsey commented on its literary merit in United States v. One Book Called "Ulysses," 5 F.Supp. 182, 184, (S.D.N.Y., 1933):

> Furthermore, "Ulysses" is an amazing tour de force when one considers the success which has been in the main achieved with such a difficult objective as Joyce set for himself. As I have stated, "Ulysses" is not an easy book to read. It is brilliant and dull, intelligible and obscure, by turns. In many places it seems to me to be disgusting, but although it contains, as I have mentioned above, many words usually considered dirty, I have not found anything that I consider to be dirt for dirt's sake. Each word of the book contributes like a bit of mosaic to the detail of the picture which Joyce is seeking to construct for his readers.

Emphasis gives force to a paragraph by the arrangement of sentences so that the most important ideas are placed at either the beginning or the end.

⚖ Rule 125.   Place important ideas at the beginning or end of the paragraph.

In Brown v. Board of Education, 347 U.S. 483, 493 (1954), the material is arranged so that it builds to an emphatic and dramatic concluding sentence:

> Today, education is perhaps the most important function of state and local governments. Compulsory school attendance laws and the great expenditures for education both demonstrate our recognition of the importance of education to our democratic society. It is required in the performance of our most basic public responsibilities, even service in the armed forces. It is the very foundation of good citizenship. Today it is a principal instrument in awakening the child to cultural values, in preparing him for later professional training, and in helping him to adjust normally to his environment. In these days, it is doubtful that any child may reasonably be expected to succeed in life if he is denied the opportunity of an education. Such an opportunity, where the state has undertaken to provide it, is a right which must be made available to all on equal terms.

Occasionally, paragraphs are constructed of only one sentence. Although one-sentence paragraphs obviously violate the rule of unity, they often serve as transitional sentences or concluding sentences. Paragraphs are often broken up into separate sentences in letters and memos in order to make better use of the white space on the page.

⚖ Rule 126.   Use one-sentence paragraphs only for transitions or emphasis.

> *Transitional sentence (paragraph):* Now we turn our attention to the facts in this case.
> *Concluding sentence (paragraph):* The appeal is dismissed for lack of a final judgment.

In addition to *unity, coherence,* and *emphasis,* there's a psychological aspect to be considered when constructing paragraphs. At first glance, your paragraph should look readable. Think for a moment about your own reaction to a page unrelieved by paragraph indentions. You may be tempted to skim over or skip entirely a very long paragraph. If you have to reread a paragraph to understand its meaning, you'll certainly be annoyed.

⚖ Rule 127.   Make your paragraphs short enough to look readable.

How short is short enough? The answer depends, of course, on the purpose of your document and the size of the page. Remember that a paragraph consuming an entire page has already lost any benefit as an organizing unit.

In briefs, memoranda, and other formal documents, try to confine your paragraphs to no more than half a double-spaced page. If your page is single-spaced, the print will appear even more dense, so try to limit your paragraphs to no more than one-fourth of the page. Of course, some paragraphs will be longer than others, so use these size recommendations only as guidelines. Keep in mind that the reader's brain needs the "relief" of white space occasionally throughout the entire page of print.

In more informal documents only one page or so in length, arrange your paragraphs to make good use of the white space on the page and present a visual balance for the eye of the reader. As a reader, you expect shorter paragraphs in informal writing, because the complexities of logical analysis are usually reserved for formal documents.

Newsletters and other communications set in print or double columns will generally require shorter paragraphs so that the column will not appear too long to the reader. For a technical approach to the visual impact of paragraphs, see "The Architecture of Type" in Roger C. Parker's *Looking Good in Print* (1990).

9

Principles of Organization

Legal writers are often faced with formidable organizational problems as they outline and plan complex legal documents such as briefs and memoranda. For a detailed discussion of considerations such as placement of questions presented, statement of facts, brief answers, and other essential components of traditional legal writing, see Chapters 3 and 4 of *Winning Words: A Guide to Persuasive Writing for Lawyers*, by Lucy V. Katz.

Because an analysis of large and complex documents is beyond the scope of this book, we've focused on some useful organizational principles to guide the reader through paragraphs and sentences. We've also included some rules about footnotes, since many readers consider the overuse of footnotes the bane of the legal profession.

⚖ Rule 128. Use organic transitions as much as possible.

Organic transitions function as useful signposts for the reader. An organic transition grows naturally from the writer's words on paper. These transitions may serve to summarize, emphasize, or even repeat key words and concepts.

> A *similar decision* was reached in the *Williams* case.
> *The Williams holding*, then, can be applied to the present case.
> From the *above analysis*, we may conclude . . .

Organic transitions, in addition to leading the reader through the text, help to focus the reader on the important issue or concept.

◣ Rule 129.   Use synthetic transitions very precisely.

Synthetic transitions add transitional elements applied by the writer to signal a change of direction or some organizational pattern. Most legal writers become familiar with synthetic transitions such as *however, therefore,* and *consequently.*

These transitions, when used sparingly and precisely, help to alert the reader to the organizational pattern of the paragraph. If they are used repeatedly throughout a document, though, readers become annoyed. A paragraph containing six sentences and five introductory transitions would be awkward and unwieldy. But some alternative words, such as those suggested below, are helpful signals to the reader.

Here are some suggestions to replace the transitions that lawyers tend to overwork.

consequently	then, thus, as a result, for that reason
however	but, by contrast, conversely, nevertheless, nonetheless, on the contrary, on the other hand, still, yet
therefore	accordingly, so, further, moreover, in addition

Choose the word that best suits the context of your sentence. Then reread your paragraph to make sure that your transitions help the reader to glide smoothly from one idea to another. If your transitional words seem to interrupt the flow of ideas on the page, delete some of them. Conversely, reexamine the overall logic of the paragraph itself; perhaps that is the problem.

🔨 Rule 130. Use descriptive headings.

This rule would be equally at home in Chapter 10, "Principles of Format," but we've included it here because we believe descriptive headings help the writer to organize material for best effect.

Legal writers learn about the importance of headings when drafting their first legal document. In fact, many courts have very specific requirements for an outline and table of contents. These outline and content headings will then become the organizational headings within the document.

You'll recognize the following as just some of the traditional headings for briefs and memoranda: Questions Presented, Brief Answer, Statement of Facts, Applicable Statutes, Discussion, Argument, and Conclusion.

These headings, and others like them (Jurisdiction, for example), provide a roadmap for your reader by indicating logical divisions in your text. In addition to providing logical and traditional separations in text, briefs must indicate the writer's position on each issue presented by the brief. Keep in mind that the meaning of this type of persuasive heading should be crystal clear to the reader.

Test for readability this heading from a lawyer's brief:

THE TRIAL COURT ERRED IN DENYING PLAINTIFF'S REQUEST FOR A DECLARATORY JUDGMENT, FINDING THAT THE DOWNZONING VIOLATED HIS CONSTITUTIONALLY PROTECTED RIGHTS AS A PROPERTY OWNER AS MORE SPECIFICALLY PLED IN PLAINTIFF'S THIRD CLAIM FOR RELIEF AND FURTHER ERRED IN REFUSING TO GRANT PLAINTIFF'S MOTION FOR JUDICIAL REVIEW PURSUANT TO C.R.C.P. 106.

In addition to the writer's failure to keep the grammatical structure of this sentence parallel, it's too long and complex to serve as a heading. This heading should function as a capsule review of the writer's position, with explanation and discussion in the section following.

Here's the way the argument should be phrased:

> THE TRIAL COURT ERRED IN DENYING PLAINTIFF'S RE-QUEST FOR A DECLARATORY JUDGMENT HOLDING THAT THE DOWNZONING VIOLATED PLAINTIFF'S CONSTITU-TIONAL RIGHTS AS A PROPERTY OWNER, AS STATED IN PLAINTIFF'S THIRD CLAIM FOR RELIEF. THE COURT FUR-THER ERRED IN REFUSING TO GRANT PLAINTIFF'S MO-TION FOR JUDICIAL REVIEW PURSUANT TO C.R.C.P. 106.

In the first sentence, the grammatical sense is now clear. The modifying clause explains that the plaintiff requested a judicial declaration about her constitutional property rights. But the caption is still misleading because it combines two distinct legal theories in a single assignment of error. The first theory deals with a constitutional issue; the second deals with the trial court's refusal to grant a motion for judicial review.

Organic headings often serve as additional subheadings and guideposts for the reader. Unlike the traditional outline headings for briefs and memoranda (Brief Summary, Argument), organic headings are taken from the actual content of the writing. For example:

> *Animals:* Heading from a residential lease agreement
> *Calculating the Remainder Interest Discount:* Heading from an estate-planning newsletter
> *Johnson's Past Disciplinary Record:* Heading from the labor union's brief in an arbitration case

These descriptive headings, in addition to insuring that the writer makes logical divisions in content, provide the reader a mental marker for the details following. In case of distractions, readers can easily find their place in the document and absorb the relevance of details.

⚖ Rule 131. Don't put essential information in footnotes.

Writers often forget that footnotes interrupt the textual material. Instead of helping the reader to understand the text, footnotes may actually serve to break up the orderly presentation of ideas.

Confronted with repeated interruptions in the discussion of a complex legal issue, readers may tire of being directed to the bottom of the page to find only additional citations or extraneous material. Some judges candidly confess to skipping footnotes in briefs. Faced with this reality, legal writers must be careful not to bury substantive material in a footnote, where it might be overlooked.

When do footnotes serve a useful purpose? Typically, the effective footnote will provide sources of authority, list recent interpretations of leading cases, or elaborate an argument already stated in the text. Footnotes should not be used to introduce a new theory or idea, nor should they contradict the main text. The Supreme Court, of course, sometimes buries the central meaning of its cases in footnotes, but judges generally do not approve of that practice by lawyers.

Below are some examples of footnotes used consistently with our rule:

> *Supplementary citation to authority:* "For more accounts of the incident, see George West, *Report on the Colorado Strike* (Washington: Government Printing Office, 1915)."
>
> *Updating case law:* "The *Martin* case was recently followed in Ellis v. Dakota Packing Co., 987 F.2d 1055 (4th Cir. 1993)."
>
> *Supporting the argument:* "The proposition that public sector strikes were illegal at common law is substantiated in leading historical studies. See, for example, Sterling Spero, *Government as Employer* (New York: Remsen Press, 1948)."

⚖ Rule 132. Keep footnotes as brief as possible.

The information in a footnote (remember, it's *nonessential* information) should be available to the reader at a glance. Unfortunately, some lawyers' footnotes are so long and complex that the reader has to absorb an argument within an argument, then flip back to the page where the footnote originated, and reread the page for the context of the main argument.

Legal writers who employ the runover footnote may be trying to subvert the court's own page limitation by cramming more single-spaced words into a lengthy footnote than a double-spaced page would allow. This is a risky practice, because some judges don't read footnotes, or avoid long ones altogether.

Footnotes are in no danger of disappearing, since they reflect a traditional and scholarly way of categorizing information. But they should be used judiciously and sparingly. Always keep your reader in mind when writing footnotes. Law review editors and perhaps even law review readers have a greater tolerance for additional sources and commentaries than do busy judges.

10

Principles of Format

Modern law offices—indeed, offices everywhere—are no longer confined to preprinted forms and typewritten documents. Because of the proliferation of word processors, legal writers now face decisions about formatting virtually every piece of writing produced. Lawyers today design and produce a variety of documents, from the traditional briefs and memoranda to newsletters and press releases. The principles that follow give some general guidelines for readability.

⚖ Rule 133. Follow the court's formal rules of format.

Courts, and even some agencies, often have very specific rules for formatting legal documents. These rules may specify a page limit, the divisions and headings to be used, and even the size and kind of paper to be submitted. Court-mandated page limitations for briefs and other documents are becoming commonplace as courts face growing case backlogs.

The Colorado Court of Appeals, for instance, has a thirty-page limitation for principal briefs and an eighteen-page limitation for reply briefs. Of course, writers may seek permission for an extension of pages, but most courts take the page limitation very seriously and become annoyed by briefs exceeding those limitations.

Judges from the federal appeals court in Chicago have been particularly tough on lawyers seeking to circumvent the fifty-page limit on appellate briefs. Quoting one of the court's previous rulings on overly long briefs, the judges said: "Litigants frequently assert the necessity of additional pages to represent their clients adequately. Overly long briefs, however, may actually hurt a party's case, making it 'far more likely that meritorious arguments will be lost amid the mass of detail.' "

⚖ Rule 134. Avoid the overuse of attention-getting graphics.

We've talked about the organizational advantages of descriptive headings in Rule 130. We noted that descriptive headings should be short and clear in order to be readily understood by the reader. There's another aspect of descriptive headings that should not be overlooked: Too many attention-getting devices may cause the reader great difficulty in getting through the heading. In the earlier rule, we gave you the heading from a lawyer's brief in all capitals only. Here is how it actually looked—all capitals, boldface type, and underlined.

THE TRIAL COURT ERRED IN DENYING PLAINTIFF'S REQUEST FOR A DECLARATORY JUDGMENT, FINDING THAT THE DOWNZONING VIOLATED HIS CONSTITUTIONALLY PROTECTED RIGHTS AS A PROPERTY OWNER AS MORE SPECIFICALLY PLED IN PLAINTIFF'S THIRD CLAIM FOR RELIEF AND FURTHER ERRED IN REFUSING TO GRANT PLAINTIFF'S MOTION FOR JUDICIAL REVIEW PURSUANT TO C.R.C.P. 106.

Now compare for readability our revised version in all capitals only.

THE TRIAL COURT ERRED IN DENYING PLAINTIFF'S REQUEST FOR A DECLARATORY JUDGMENT HOLDING THAT THE DOWNZONING VIOLATED PLAINTIFF'S CONSTITUTIONAL RIGHTS AS A PROPERTY OWNER, AS STATED IN PLAINTIFF'S THIRD CLAIM FOR RELIEF. THE COURT FURTHER ERRED IN REFUSING TO GRANT PLAINTIFF'S MOTION FOR JUDICIAL REVIEW PURSUANT TO C.R.C.P. 106.

Although it's traditional to place issue or argument headings in all capitals, it's more difficult for the reader to comprehend text written in that manner. The eye needs the relief of lowercase letters mixed with uppercase letters in order to comprehend words at a glance. Readability experts say that more than a few words written in all capitals will slow reading speed significantly. In addition, underlining interferes with the reader's ability to recognize the shapes of words, and boldface type is hard to read. The combination of graphic devices, including underlining, will produce a difficult-to-read text at just the point where the reader's utmost attention is desired.

Since most of today's law offices have computers and word processors for processing documents, writers have a variety of graphic design choices to make, including a variety of available typefaces. We believe every office needs a source book for technical information on desktop publishing, such as Roger C. Parker's *Looking Good in Print*.

✎ Rule 135. Use bullets or dashes for informal listings.

Legal writers are familiar with detailed outlines and numerical listings. Statutes, contracts, and various other legal documents are full of numbers and letters denoting listings that may be quite complex. These letters and numerals serve a very useful function of providing discrete segments of information to which a reader may refer—for example, "See paragraph 2 (a) (ii)."

In less formal documents, however, listings may be formatted with introductory visual devices called *bullets* or with dashes made with a typewriter keyboard. These visual devices have become quite popular in the business world because they pro vide the reader with a quickly comprehensible visual display of ideas or items.

Legal writers arc also using these informal listings to help readers recognize and remember sequential items, especially when the order of importance isn't essential. Informal listings are helpful to readers of letters, newsletters, and office memoranda. One justice of a state supreme court told us he'd be thrilled to see such an organizing device appear on the pages of voluminous briefs. He was obviously alluding to the utility of informal listings in providing a break-up of text on the page and a focus for the writer's ideas.

Be sure to write your listings in parallel grammatical form for reading ease. Use all verbs or all nouns at the beginning, for example, to help maintain rhythm and readability.

Here is a list of the three operating principles we tried to keep in mind when preparing this book. We've arranged these principles as an example of an informal, bulleted list.

Legal writers should use

- ordinary language unless a term of art is necessary
- standard rules of grammar and syntax
- simple and clear language for persuasion

Notice how these three elements gain emphasis from their placement. Run-on in a sentence, they would attract far less attention from the reader. Notice also how we've used informal punctuation. If we had employed a more formal listing, we would have placed a colon after "Legal writers should use *the following*," numerals before the three sentence elements, commas after the first two elements in our series, and the word "and" at the end of the second element. The informality of our bulleted listing has saved us from doing all that, and we've gained a cleaner-looking listing without all the punctuation.

Glossary

Adjective

A word used to modify or limit the meaning of a noun or pronoun.

white, young, dull, wet

Adjective Clause

A clause used to modify a noun or pronoun in the manner of an adjective.

The book, *which was soiled and torn,* remained on the shelf.

Adverb

A word used to modify a verb, an adjective, or another adverb.

quickly, too, very, then, up, down

Antecedent

The noun to which a pronoun refers.

She picked up the *ball* and threw it. (*Ball* is the antecedent of *it.*)

Appositive

A noun that further describes the noun that comes before it.

Susan Spiegel, *the lawyer,* tried the case. (*Lawyer* is in apposition to *Susan Spiegel.*)

Article

The word *the* is the definite article; the words *a* and *an* are indefinite articles. *A* is used before words beginning with a consonant sound, *an* before words beginning with a vowel sound.

a brief
an opinion

Auxiliary

A verb used to assist in forming other verbs. Words such as *be, can, do, go, have, may, must, shall,* and *will* are auxiliaries (or helping verbs).

He *has* found the key

Case

The relation of a noun or pronoun to other words in the sentence as shown by inflectional form or position.

The subject of a verb is in the *nominative case.*

She is ambitious.

The object of a verb or preposition is in the *objective case.*

Give *him* the book.

A noun or pronoun that denotes possession is in the *possessive case.*

This file is *his.*

Clause

A portion of a sentence that contains a subject and a verb. The following sentence contains one dependent (subordinate) and one independent (main) clause.

When the police arrived, the victim was unconscious.

Comparison

The change in the form of an adjective or adverb to indicate the degree of quality, quantity, or manner. The three degrees are positive, comparative, and superlative.

eagerly, more eagerly, most eagerly

Complex Sentence

A sentence containing one main clause and one or more dependent clauses.

When they arrived at the courthouse, they noticed the halls were empty.

Compound Sentence

A sentence containing two or more main clauses, each of which could function as a complete sentence.

The whistle blew, and *everyone stopped working.*

Conjugation

The inflectional changes in the verb to indicate person, number, tense, voice, and mood.

I *am* tired. (first person singular present tense)
We *are* overworked. (first person plural present tense)
I *was* exhausted. (first person singular past tense)
It *was recommended* that I take a vacation. (passive voice)
I wish I *were* on the beach. (subjunctive mood)

Conjunction

A word that connects words, phrases, or clauses. Coordinating conjunctions connect words, phrases, and clauses of equal rank.

for, and, nor, but, or, yet, so

Subordinating conjunctions connect subordinate clauses with main clauses.

although, because, unless, when, while

Conjunctive Adverb

A word that is used sometimes as an adverb and sometimes as a conjunctive.

accordingly, besides, hence, however, moreover, still, thus, yet.

Construction

The grammatical use of a word in a sentence.

Copulative (or Linking) Verbs

A verb used to link the subject with the predicate complement and expressing the relation between subject and complement. *Is, was, becomes, looks, tastes, smells, feels,* and *sounds* are common copulative verbs.

Finite Verb

A verb or verb form that is capable of making an independent assertion concerning the subject.

The ship *sank.* The ship *is sinking.*

Infinitives, gerunds, and participles, which are nonfinite forms of the verb, are incapable of making an independent assertion.

Gender

The classification of nouns and some pronouns as masculine, feminine, common, and neuter.

masculine: man, he
feminine: woman, she
neuter: pencil, baby

Gerund

A word ending in *ing* that acts as both a verb and a noun. The gerund resembles a verb in taking an object and in being modified by an adverb. It resembles a noun in that it can perform the chief functions of a noun and can be modified by an adjective.

> *Rowing* is splendid exercise. (noun)
> We enjoyed the *singing*. (object of verb)

Idiom

An expression that is peculiar to a particular language and acceptable in daily usage.

> *How's it going?*
> The *old boy* won't tolerate it.

Independent Element

A word or group of words not having any grammatical connection with the sentence in which it stands:

> I believe, *George*, that you will be successful.
> The entire committee, *we trust*, will be present.
> *Dusk having descended*, the guns became silent.

Infinitive

A verbal form preceded by *to* and used on occasion as a noun, an adjective, or an adverb. The *to* is often omitted after certain verbs:

> She urged him *to leave* at once. She helped *(to) write* the interrogatory.
> *Used as a noun:* To live courageously is wise.
> *Used as an adjective:* Our desire *to travel* was overwhelming.
> *Used as an adverb:* He does not go to the gym *to exercise*.

Interjection

A word that expresses emotion and that has no syntactic relation to other words in the sentence.

Ah, now I understand.
Ouch! That really hurts.

Intransitive, Transitive

A verb is transitive or intransitive according to its use in a sentence.

A verb that requires a direct object to complete its meaning is a *transitive verb.*

He *sells* books.

A verb that does not require a direct object to complete its meaning is an *intransitive* verb.

He *studied* diligently.

Many verbs may be used transitively or intransitively.

She *drove* slowly. (intransitive)
She *drove* her automobile. (transitive)

Modifier

A word, phrase, or clause that changes the meaning of the word to which it is grammatically related.

He enjoys *sweet* grapes.
She criticizes *freely*.

Mood (Mode)

The set of inflectional forms and verb phrases used to represent the action of the verb in a certain mode. There are three moods.

The *indicative* mood is used to ask a question or state a fact.

Did he study?
He studied.

The *imperative* mood is used to express a request or give a command.

Please, speak clearly.
Don't move.

The *subjunctive* mood is used to express a condition contrary to fact, a doubt, a wish, or a desire.

> If I were you, I'd work hard.
> I wish he were my instructor.

Nominative

The case of the noun or pronoun when it functions as either the subject or complement of a linking verb.

> She is the prosecutor.
> The prosecutor is she.

Nonrestrictive

A nonessential modifier. A clause or phrase that could be omitted without changing the basic meaning of the sentence.

> Latin, *which is now considered a dead language,* is important in many ways to the legal profession.

Noun

A word used to denote a person, place, or thing.
A *proper* noun names a particular person, place, or thing.

> *George, England, Lincoln Monument*

A *common* noun names any one of the members of a class of persons, places, or things.

> *woman, village, table*

A *collective* noun names a group.

> *club, choir, commission, jury, company, team*

An *abstract* noun names a quality or an idea.

> *brilliance, truth, compassion*

A *concrete* noun names something that can be perceived by any of the senses.

> *apple, lake, rose, child*

Number

The change in the form of a noun, a pronoun, or a verb to indicate whether it designates one (*singular*) or more than one (*plural*).

Object

A word, phrase, or subordinate clause used to indicate the person or thing affected by the action of a transitive verb, or the noun or pronoun used to complete the meaning of a preposition.

The person or thing directly affected by the action of a verb is called the *direct object*.

> I called *her*.

The person or thing indirectly affected by the action of the verb is called the *indirect object*.

> She handed *me* the pen.

The noun or pronoun used to complete the meaning of a preposition is referred to as the *object of a preposition*.

> He strolled along the *lane*.

Parenthetical Expression

An expression inserted in a sentence that would be grammatically complete without it.

Participle

A verb form that functions like both an adjective and a verb.

> The results were *encouraging*.
> The child, *encouraged* by her father, rode the unicycle.

Parts of Speech

The classification of words according to their function in sentences. In order to determine what part of speech a word is, ask yourself how it is used in the sentence. There are eight generally recognized parts of speech: *nouns, pronouns, adjectives, verbs, adverbs, prepositions, conjunctions,* and *interjections.*

Person

The change in the form of a pronoun or a verb to show first person, the speaker (*I* am); second person, the person spoken to (*you* are); and third person, the person spoken about (*he* or *she* is).

Phrase

A group of words not containing a subject or a predicate that functions as a single part of speech.

> *Gerund phrase: In talking,* he found solace.
> *Infinitive phrase:* George likes *to read his poems.*
> *Participial phrase: Looking to the south,* he saw a hill.
> *Prepositional phrase: In the evening* is the time to relax.
> *Verb phrase:* She *has been gone* a long time.

Predicate Complement

The word or words used to complete the meaning of a copulative linking verb and to describe or identify the subject of the verb. It may take the form of a noun, a noun clause, a pronoun, an adjective, an adjective phrase, an infinitive, or a gerund.

> Harry is his *uncle.* (noun)
> His advice is *that they study diligently.* (noun clause)
> It is *she.* (pronoun)
> They are *alert.* (adjective)
> The target is *out of range.* (adjective phrase)
> To participate is *to enjoy.* (infinitive)
> Listening is *learning.* (gerund)

Predicate complements are also referred to as *subject complements, predicate nominatives,* and *predicate adjectives.*

Preposition

A word used to show the relation of a noun or pronoun to some other word in the sentence.

The lion is *in* the cage.

Pronoun

A word used in place of a noun.

Restrictive

An essential modifier. A clause or phrase that could not be omitted without changing the basic meaning of the sentence.

The dog *that bit me* is rabid.

Sentence

A group of words composed of a subject and a predicate and not grammatically dependent on any words outside itself.

Subject

A noun or pronoun that names the person or thing about which an assertion is made.

Syntax

The study of the rules for forming grammatical sentences in a language.

Tense

The several sets of forms and combinations that a verb has when it represents action as occurring at different points of time are called its tenses. There are six tenses: *present, past, future, present perfect, past perfect, future perfect.*

Present: She testifies.
Past: She testified.
Future: She will testify.
Present perfect: She has testified.

Past perfect: She had testified.
Future perfect: She will have testified.

Verb

A word capable of making an assertion concerning a person or thing.

Verbal

A word derived from a verb, but used as a noun or an adjective. The verbals are *infinitive, gerund,* and *participle.*

Voice

The change in the form of a verb to indicate whether the subject acts (*active voice*) or is acted upon (*passive voice*).

Recommended Sources

Books and Articles on Legal Writing

Aldisert, Ruggero J. *Opinion Writing*. St. Paul: West Publishing Co., 1990.

Alterman, Irving. *Plain and Accurate Style in Court Papers*. Philadelphia: American Law Institute—American Bar Association Committee on Continuing Professional Education, 1987.

American Bar Association, Appellate Judges Conference, *Judicial Opinion Writing Manual*. St. Paul: West Publishing Co., 1991.

Bablich, William A. "Writing to Win: Briefs Should Communicate—Not Obfuscate, Metagrobolize, Obnuliate or Bedim." *The Compleat Lawyer*, vol. 5, 1988, p. 8.

Calleros, Charles R. *Legal Method and Legal Writing*. Boston: Little Brown and Co., 1990.

Charrow, Veda R., and Myra K. Erhardt. *Clear & Effective Legal Writing*. Boston: Little Brown and Co., 1986.

Dernbach, John C., and Richard V. Singleton II. *A Practical Guide to Legal Writing and Legal Method*. Littleton, CO: Fred B. Rothman & Co., 1981.

Felsenfeld, Carl, and Alan Siegel. *Writing Contracts in Plain English*. St. Paul: West Publishing Co., 1981.

Goldstein, Tom, and Jethro K. Lieberman. *The Lawyer's Guide to Writing Well*. Berkeley: University of California Press, 1991.

Katz, Lucy V. *Winning Words: A Guide to Persuasive Writing for Lawyers*. New York: Harcourt Brace Jovanovich, Inc., 1986.

Mellinkoff, David. *Legal Writing: Sense and Nonsense*. St. Paul: West Publishing Co., 1982.

115

Squires, Lynn B., and Marjorie D. Rombauer. *Legal Writing in a Nutshell*. St. Paul: West Publishing Co., 1982.

Stark, Steven. "Why Lawyers Can't Write." *Harvard Law Review*, vol. 97, 1984, p. 1389.

Wydick, Richard C. *Plain English for Lawyers*. 2d ed. Durham, NC: Carolina Academic Press, 1985.

Younger, Irving. *Persuasive Writing*. The Professional Education Group, Inc., 1990.

Legal Reference Books

Black's Law Dictionary. 6th ed. St. Paul: West Publishing Co., 1990.

Burton, William C. *Legal Thesaurus*. New York: Macmillan Publishing Co., 1980.

Dworsky, Alan L. *User's Guide to The Bluebook*. Littleton, CO: Fred B. Rothman & Co., 1991.

A Uniform System of Citation. 15th ed. Cambridge, MA: Harvard Law Review Association, 1991.

General Writing and Reference Books

Blake, Gary, and Robert W. Bly. *The Elements of Business Writing*. New York: Macmillan Publishing Co., 1991.

The Merriam-Webster Concise Handbook for Writers. Springfield, MA: Merriam-Webster, Inc., 1991.

The Merriam-Webster Dictionary of English Usage. Springfield, MA: Merriam-Webster, Inc., 1989.

Parker, Roger C. *Looking Good in Print*. 2d ed. Chapel Hill, NC: Ventana Press, Inc., 1990.

Shaw, Harry. *Punctuate It Right!* 2d ed. New York: Harper Collins, 1993.

Strunk, William, Jr., and E. B. White. *The Elements of Style*. 3d rev. ed. New York: Macmillan Publishing Co., 1981.

U.S. Government Printing Office: Style Manual. Washington: U.S. Government Printing Office, 1984.

Index

About the Authors

Martha Faulk is a former college English instructor and consultant in business writing. After returning to school to receive a law degree, she practiced law as a sole practitioner. She now conducts continuing legal education seminars in legal writing for state and local bar associations and does consulting work with law offices and law firms. She lives in Fort Collins, Colorado.

Readers wishing more information may reach Martha Faulk through The Professional Education Group, Inc., 12401 Minnetonka Boulevard, Minnetonka, Minnesota 55305-3969 (800-229-2531).

Irving M. Mehler is a retired lawyer and law professor. The author of *Effective Legal Communication* and former Editor of Opinions for the Supreme Court of Colorado, he published many articles in legal journals and legal newspapers during his distinguished career. Mr. Mehler lives in Denver, Colorado, where he does volunteer work with the aged and infirm.